Social Processes in Children's Learning

This book is about children's learning and problem-solving behaviour. It reflects the increasingly close integration seen in recent years between social and cognitive approaches to researching the learning process. In particular, Paul Light and Karen Littleton examine the ways in which interactions between children influence learning outcomes. They begin by placing this topic in a broad theoretical and empirical context and go on to present a substantial series of their own experimental studies, which focus on children of late primary and early secondary school age. These investigations address peer facilitation of problem solving, social comparison effects on learning and social context effects upon the interpretation of tasks. Many of the studies involve computer-based learning but the findings have implications both for classroom practice and the understanding of the learning process.

This book will be a valuable tool for researchers, teachers and practitioners interested in the social processes of children's learning.

PAUL LIGHT is Pro-Vice-Chancellor of Bournemouth University, and has held teaching and research posts in psychology at the Universities of Cambridge and Southampton. He has published in a wide range of journals including *Quarterly Journal of Experimental Psychology, Journal of Experimental Child Psychology, Child Development* and *Journal of Child Psychology and Psychiatry*. His books include *The Development of Social Sensitivity* (1979); *Social Cognition* (with G. Butterworth, 1982); *Children of Social Worlds* (with M. Richards, 1986); *Learning to Think* (with S. Sheldon and M. Woodhead, 1991); and *Context and Cognition* (with G. Butterworth, 1992).

KAREN LITTLETON currently holds an ESRC personal research fellowship at the Open University. She has published in a range of journals including *European Journal of Psychology of Education, Cognition and Instruction,* and *Educational Psychology*. In addition, she has edited *Learning with Computers* (with P. Light, 1999); and *Cultural Worlds of Early Childhood, Learning Relationships in the Classroom* and *Making Sense of Social Development* (all 1998 and 1999 and all with M. Woodhead & D. Faulkner).

Cambridge Studies in Cognitive and Perceptual Development

The aim of this series is to provide a scholarly forum for current theoretical and empirical issues in cognitive and perceptual development. As the twentieth century draws to a close, the field is no longer dominated by monolithic theories. Contemporary explanations build on the combined influences of biological, cultural, contextual and ecological factors in well-defined research domains. In the field of cognitive devlopment, cultural and situational factors are widely recognised as influencing the emergence and forms of reasoning in children. In perceptual development, the field has moved beyond the oposition of 'innate' and 'acquired' to suggest a continuous role for perception in the acquistion of knowledge. These approaches and issues will all be reflected in the series which will also address such important research themes as the indissociable link betweeen perception and action in the developing motor system, the relationship between preceptual and cognitive development to modern ideas on the development of the brain, the significance of developmental processes themselves, dynamic systems theory and contemporary work in the psychodynamic tradition, especially as it relates to the foundations of self-knowledge.

Titles published in the series

1. *Imitation in Infancy*
Jacqueline Nadel and George Butterworth

2. *Learning to Read and Write: A Cross-Linguistic Perspective*
Margaret Harris and Giyoo Hatano

3. *Children's Understanding of Biology and Health*
Michael Siegal and Candida Peterson

Forthcoming titles

Nobuo Masataka
The Onset of Language

Social Processes in Children's Learning

Paul Light and Karen Littleton

Bournemouth University and *The Open University*

CAMBRIDGE
UNIVERSITY PRESS

PUBLISHED BY THE PRESS SYNDICATE OF THE UNIVERSITY OF CAMBRIDGE
The Pitt Building, Trumpington Street, Cambridge, United Kingdom

CAMBRIDGE UNIVERSITY PRESS
The Edinburgh Building, Cambridge, CB2 2RU, UK
http://www.cup.cam.ac.uk
40 West 20th Street, New York, NY 10011–4211, USA   http://www.cup.org
10 Stamford Road, Oakleigh, Melbourne 3166, Australia

© Paul Light and Karen Littleton 1999

First published 1999

Printed in the United Kingdom at the University Press, Cambridge

Typeset in Plantin 10/12pt [VN]

A catalogue record for this book is available from the British Library

Library of Congress Cataloguing in Publication data

Light, Paul.
Social processes in children's learning / Paul Light and Karen Littleton.
    p.   cm. – (Cambridge studies in cognitive and perceptual development)
Includes bibliographical references.
ISBN 0 521 59308 5 (hardback) ISBN 0 521 59691 2 (paperback)
1. Learning–Social aspects.   2. Social interaction in children.   3. Group work
in education.   I. Littleton, Karen.   II. Title.   III. Series.
LB1060.L533 1999
370.15'23–dc21   99–19464   CIP

ISBN 0 521 59308 5 hardback
ISBN 0 521 59691 2 paperback

To Vivienne and Ian

Contents

Figures

Preface

Two decades ago, in a monograph on 'The Development of Social Sensitivity', one of us concluded that: 'The way is open for much more detailed and delicate study of the relationship between cognitive development and experience in a social environment' (Light, 1979, p. 117). Research in the ensuing years has indeed added greatly to our understanding of this relationship, and the purpose of the present volume is to explore one particular aspect of it, namely the relationship between children's learning and their experience of interaction with peers.

In common with a great deal of the research undertaken in developmental and social psychology over the last twenty years, our subject matter can be embraced by the term 'social-cognition'. However, this term encompasses a variety of very different research enterprises. On the one hand, we have research which is concerned with understanding of social phenomena. This encompasses perception and understanding of self and other, understanding others' intentions and emotions, and more generally the emergence of a 'theory of mind'. On the other hand, we have research which examines the ways in which more general aspects of cognitive development are shaped by social interactions. Here we see traditional topics of cognitive developmental research such as reasoning and concept formation analysed in social-interactional terms.

As Butterworth and Light (1982) observed, the relationships between these various strands of research on socio-cognitive development have often been poorly defined and confusing. Butterworth, in that volume, observed that: 'theories have been imported from cognitive development on the one hand and social psychology on the other, to lie in an uneasy relationship' (1982, p. 5). The appearance fifteen years later of a mammoth undergraduate text on 'Developmental Social Psychology' (Durkin, 1995) reflects the extent to which the rapprochement between developmental and social psychology has progressed, but Durkin still describes the difficulties faced by the enterprise as intimidating.

Durkin draws a similar distinction to that drawn above, between social cognition as concerned with 'cognition *about* social phenomena' and social cognition as concerned with 'cognition *as a product of* social interaction'. The present volume addresses social cognition in this second sense, drawing substantially upon research which we have conducted with various European colleagues. More particularly, our focus will be upon *social interactions between learners* as an influence upon learning.

The capacity for collaborative learning is widely, and perhaps increasingly, seen as a key feature of human cognitive development. For example, in a major *Behavioral and Brain Sciences* (*BBS*) target article, Tomasello, Kruger and Ratner (1993) address the age old question of 'what's so special about humans?' Their answer is that what is most distinctive about humans is the possession of a culture. Culture is defined in terms of material artefacts, social institutions, behavioural traditions and languages, all having the capacity to change over time. Their hypothesis is that underlying all this distinctively human paraphernalia of culture is a fundamental characteristic of human learning, namely a capacity for *socially grounded* learning. Such learning is marked by the fact that it involves not just learning how to do things, but also coming to understand situations in terms of the purposes and intentions of others, and appropriating their points of view upon shared activities.

Tomasello *et al.* envisage a progression from imitation through instruction to collaborative learning, the capacity for which is seen as emerging in the early school years and as being a vital (perhaps *the* vital) ingredient in cultural learning. After all, they observe, 'Human children are born into a world in which most of the tasks they are expected to master are collaborative inventions' (1993, p. 508). They put the spotlight on the social sensitivity of the learner, attempting to establish the preconditions for cultural learning at the level of the individual. They ask, in effect, 'what do learners have to be capable of to engage in cultural learning?'.

This approach is open to the obvious criticism (taken up by many of the commentators on the *BBS* article) that it treats the individual as 'prior' to culture. The counter-view is that cultural learning is itself a product of culture. After all, opportunities to engage in imitation, instruction and collaboration are themselves afforded or constrained by what the culture offers, for example by way of apprenticeship or schooling. It may be going too far to claim that culture creates the child in its own image, but the relationship is surely at least a bidirectional one.

At some level, the efficacy of collaborative learning, for example, must depend upon the individual's developing psychological model of others. At the same time, the development of such psychological models must be dependent upon social experience. We are thus dealing with a dynamic system of transactions. Disciplinary traditions vary in the ways in which they conceptualise the relationships involved, but, whether one starts from the standpoint of the individual developing learner or of the social and cultural order, it is apparent that social processes mediate learning in crucial ways.

The role of interaction in learning is an issue of obvious relevance to education as well as to psychology. The work described in this volume draws from both literatures. Educational interest in the potential of group work for fostering children's learning has a long pedigree, a useful review of which can be found in Kutnick and Rogers (1994). Educational reports on both sides of the Atlantic, certainly since the 1920s and 1930s, have lent encouragement to small group work in the classroom. In the UK, the Plowden Report of 1967 was in part responsible for a shift from whole class teaching towards small group teaching at primary school level. The Report advocated groupwork for a variety of reasons, some to do with classroom organisation and efficiency, some to do with socialisation, and some to do with specifically cognitive benefits of this mode of learning. Today, classrooms in the UK and throughout much of the developed world typically have children sitting around tables in small groups, rather than sitting in individual desks in serried ranks, facing the teacher.

The physical arrangement of the classroom can be deceptive, however. The children sitting in these groups may be working separately at different tasks. Whole class teaching also can and does go on within such classrooms. Observational classroom research in the UK indicates that teachers rarely assign tasks that depend upon collaborative modes of learning, and that rather little in the way of pedagogically effective groupwork actually occurs (Bennett, Desforges, Cockburn and Wilkinson, 1984; Galton and Williamson, 1992; Tizard, Blatchford, Burke, Farquhar and Plewis, 1988). However, there is at least one aspect of the curriculum in relation to which groupwork has seen something of a renaissance in recent years, namely the use of computers.

A combination of hardware shortages and a lack of confidence amongst many teachers may have conspired to favour a pupil-centred, small group approach to learning with computers. A survey of UK primary schools in the mid-1980s found that computers were predominantly used by two or three children at a time (Jackson, Fletcher and Messer, 1986). Indeed many of the teachers responding to that survey saw one of the main educational benefits of computers as being the fact that they were particularly good at supporting groupwork. With computers it is also often the case that some of the children in a class have considerable expertise gained outside school, thus disturbing the usual 'teacher-centred' distribution of expertise (Shrock and Stepp, 1991).

Despite the fact that the typical desktop computer seems to have been designed for a single user, classroom observations of computer use have long emphasised the potential of computers to support effective learning interactions (e.g. Cummings, 1985). Relatively autonomous groupwork around computer resources seems to many observers to offer opportunities for genuine discussion between pupils of a kind which is hard to sustain in other classroom contexts (Scanlon, Issroff and Murphy, 1998). The social dimensions of children's learning interactions around computers will emerge as a major focus of this volume.

The role of discussion and disagreement between peers has long exercised researchers concerned with the role of social interaction in children's cognitive development and learning. As we shall discuss in more detail in the first chapter of the book, Piaget has played a key role in shaping the agenda for developmental psychology in this area. Suspicious of any suggestion that intellectual development results from 'transmission' of knowledge and understanding from experts to novices, Piaget (e.g. 1932) downplayed the importance of adult–child interchanges in favour of an emphasis on the productive potential of peer interactions. He argued that the egocentrism which so limited the thinking of preschool and early school-age children could be overcome through encounters with different points of view. Differences of points of view between *peers* he saw as having particular value as they demand resolution, whereas differences of view between a child and an adult may result simply in compliance.

Neo-Piagetian developments of these ideas, associated most notably with the work of Doise and colleagues (e.g. Doise, 1990; Doise and Mugny, 1984) have bought the concept of 'socio-cognitive conflict' to prominence, and we shall have a good deal to say about it in the pages that follow. But through other concepts, such as 'social marking', Doise recognised that the social dimensions of learning interactions extend far beyond the immediate face-to-face encounter. The wider social world of rules, conventions and social etiquette impinges in a host of more or less subtle ways on the learning situation, which is thus in an important sense 'social' even when no-one else is present.

This wider sense in which intellectual development is a fundamentally social process was explicitly addressed by Vygotsky, whose rather fragmentary writings (e.g. Vygotsky (1931) 1990) have come to be regarded as seminal in this field of research. Vygotsky offered an account of some of the mutually adjustive properties which characterise effective teaching/learning interactions, building on concepts such as the zone of proximal development. This has helped to foster a tradition of experimental research on effective strategies for teaching and learning which has contributed in turn to the development of computer-based intelligent tutoring systems (Wood and Wood, 1996). It has also provided the basis for an approach to understanding how peer interaction can facilitate learning and problem solving. This highlights processes of joint construction of an appropriate representation of the problem and its solution, most notably through discussion (Mercer, 1995).

On another level, Vygotsky offered a starting point for a wider theoretical development which has come to be known as 'cultural psychology' (Crook, 1994; Cole, 1996). Crook uses the biological analogy of a 'culture' as a *medium* in which living material (bacteria, tissue cells, or whatever) can be supported and 'grown'. In a similar way, human culture is conceptualised as a medium which supports the development of thinking.

Cultural psychology focuses on thinking and reasoning as activities which take place in particular situations. This approach has come together with influences from anthropology (Lave and Wenger, 1991) and cognitive science (Suchman, 1987) to form the basis of what is now widely referred to as the 'situated learning' approach. Here learning is considered to be an intrinsic and inseparable aspect of participation in the various 'communities of practice' that make up a society.

All of these very diverse disciplinary, sub-disciplinary and multi-disciplinary perspectives see development and learning as dependent in one way or another upon the nexus of social relationships within which they occur. Many of them suggest that interactions between learners, as well as between teachers and learners, may have an important and formative role. In the chapters that follow, some of these perspectives will be explored in greater detail than others. The research evidence to be presented at times may lend itself to explanation in terms of one approach rather than another. But the different positions sketched here are not in conflict, or at least not in the sense that if one is right the others are necessarily wrong. All of them offer a case for taking child–child interaction seriously in the context of development and learning. The present volume affords us the opportunity both to pull together a considerable body of empirical research on this topic that we and our colleagues have been directly involved in, and also to set this work within the wider context of contemporary research in the field.

Acknowledgements

The writing of this volume was made possible by Economic and Social Research Council Fellowship awards to both authors (Award numbers: H52427501595 and H52427000994). Carole Kershaw and Lynda Preston gave invaluable help in preparing the manuscript for publication. Ian Wallhead and Simeon Yates kindly reproduced the figures. The empirical research on which the volume is based was supported by project grants from the ESRC, the Leverhulme Trust and the Nuffield Foundation. Other members of the research teams included Martin Glachan, Christopher Colbourn, Richard Joiner, Peter Barnes, David Messer, Agnes Blaye, Maria Silvia Barbieri and Annerieke Oosterwegel. The research also involved many schools and many hundreds of children, without whose willing and unrewarded cooperation none of the research could have been conducted. Our sincere thanks to them all.

Figures 4.1 and 4.2 are reprinted with permission from Springer-Verlag. These figures originally appeared in *Computer Supported Collaborative Learning* (1995), edited by Claire O'Malley.

Figure 4.5 is reprinted with permission from Carfax Publishing Limited. This figure originally appeared in *Educational Psychology* (1998), Volume 18, Number 3.

1 Peer interaction and learning: perspectives and starting points

Introduction

This chapter will set the scene for those that follow by going back to the 1970s to examine some of the strands of theory and empirical research which converged around the question of when and how peer interaction can facilitate children's understanding and learning. Starting with social learning theory, we shall develop a focus on the concept of socio-cognitive conflict as an engine of mental development, a concept that owes its origins to Piaget, via Doise and colleagues. The Piagetian origins of this idea are reflected in the selection of tasks in these early studies, and this in turn gives rise to certain problems in terms of the interpretation of some of the experimental findings. This consideration will take us on a slight detour in the course of this chapter, raising issues to be returned to later. The latter part of the chapter will be given over to an account of the series of experimental studies of peer facilitation of children's problem solving which marked our own initial engagement with this field of research.

Modelling success: the social learning theory approach

As inheritors of the behaviourist approach to learning, social learning theories exerted a strong influence upon the psychology of child development in the 1970s. Such theories saw *modelling* as a key formative process in cognitive as well as other aspects of development. Thus any facilitative effects of child–child interaction in learning were construed largely in terms of processes of imitation or modelling.

Studies were conducted in which children's performance on various cognitive tasks was assessed before and after they had watched other children performing the same tasks. Many of the tasks in question were drawn from the Piagetian repertoire, because social learning theorists were setting themselves against Piagetian constructivist explanations which they saw as unduly individualistic in emphasis (e.g. Murray, 1974; Rosenthal and Zimmerman, 1972). Such studies did provide some evidence that children who initially performed at 'pre-operational' levels on tasks such as conservation of quantity could be induced to give operational judgements on such tasks simply by being required to observe another child who offered such judgements. From a Piagetian point of view, however, such demonstrations were unconvincing since they did not offer evidence that the children concerned were able either to justify or to generalise these 'operational' judgements.

Other studies within this tradition went beyond passive observation to examine the effects of actual interaction between 'pre-operational' and 'operational' children in the context of such tasks (e.g. Miller and Brownell, 1975; Silverman and Geiringer, 1973). Here again, it was possible to show that the pre-operational children did tend to make progress, and in this case with some evidence that the children concerned could produce their own justifications for their new operational judgements.

However, in the interaction studies, it was harder to tie such progress to the child's exposure to a partner who 'modelled' the correct conclusion. A different kind of interpretation was developed in relation to essentially similar studies by researchers working within a 'constructivist' tradition.

Construction of understanding through socio-cognitive conflict

Piaget's own early writings (most notably, Piaget, 1932) offered an argument for the potential productivity of peer interaction in relation to cognitive development, and especially in relation to the achievement of concrete operational modes of thought in the early school years. Piaget saw the pre-school child's egocentrism as presenting the major obstacle to achievement of operational thinking. Such thinking required 'decentration', the ability to take account of multiple points of view, and more generally, multiple covarying factors in a given situation. Pre-schoolers tended to fix on the first relevant factor they identified, and to answer entirely in terms of that. What the child needed in order to progress was something which disturbed this 'centration'. Exposure to someone else who saw things differently, in a situation which called for resolution of the conflicting responses, was seen as providing just this kind of disturbance.

Importantly, Piaget considered that inequalities of power and status were inimical to the effectiveness of this process. If children were exposed to the response of a powerful figure such as an adult, they would be unlikely to take issue with it. Rather, they would tend to ignore it if possible, and comply with it if not. In the case of exposure to a differing point of view from an equal, however, the social dynamics of the situation would create a pressure towards resolution of differences: 'Criticism is born of discussion and discussion is only possible amongst equals' (Piaget, 1932, p. 409). Even if the second child's answer was as wrong as that of the first, the attempt to resolve their partial and 'centred' solutions would be likely to result in the achievement of a higher level, more decentred representation which could embrace what was correct in both of the initial offerings.

In the mid-1970s, Doise and colleagues in Geneva conducted a series of experiments on the effects of peer interaction on the transition to operational modes of thinking in five to seven-year-olds (Doise, Mugny, and Perret-Clermont, 1975, 1976; Mugny and Doise, 1978). These studies used a variety of Piagetian 'concrete operations' tasks, a favourite being a 'village' task based loosely on Piaget's famous 'three mountains' task (Piaget and Inhelder, 1956). Here, model buildings were arranged on a baseboard to form a little village. The buildings are oriented in relation to a fixed mark on the baseboard, depicting, say, the village pond. The whole arrangement sat on a tabletop in front of the child. To the side of the child was another table, with an identical baseboard, but perhaps oriented differently in relation to the child. The child's task was to use a replica set of model buildings to recreate exactly the *same* village on this second table. The task is more or less difficult depending upon the relative orientations of the two baseboards. Where a rotation relative to self is involved, pre-operational children will typically fail to take account of the reorientations necessary to preserve the relationships between the buildings and the fixed mark.

Children were first tested individually on the task, to get a 'pre-test' measure of performance. In a second session, perhaps a week later, children were given another opportunity to do similar tasks, but this time some of them worked in pairs or small groups while others worked alone. Assignment to conditions was essentially random, although in some studies allocations to particular groupings was on the basis of pre-test performance. Sometimes, when the 'village' task was used, the children were put in different positions relative to the tables, so that the necessary transformation was easier for one child than for the other. In a third session, a week later again, all of the children were given a post-test individually.

Through such studies, Doise and his colleagues were able to show that children of slightly different pre-test levels, working together in dyads or triads, tended to perform at a higher level when working as a group than children working alone. More importantly, this benefit carried over to the children's individual post-test performances. In other words, the extent of pre- to post-test progress was significantly greater for those children who had worked in pairs in the second session than for those who had worked alone.

Large differences between the children in terms of their pre-test levels were associated with less progress than small differences in initial ability (Doise and Mugny, 1984). Even children who showed identical levels of pre-test performance could benefit from working together if steps were taken to ensure that they would come up with conflicting responses. Thus, with the village task, Doise and colleagues arranged for such children to occupy different spatial positions relative to the array. This meant that their 'egocentric' responses would ensure that they came into conflict about where to place the buildings, even though they were both reasoning in the same way. Children paired under these conditions made more gains than similar children working on the tasks on their own.

Doise and colleagues interpreted their findings in terms of socio-cognitive conflict. The children in the pair or small group conditions found themselves confronted with solutions which conflicted with their own. This conflict, and the socially engendered need to resolve it, prompts the children to re-examine their own initial responses, and may lead them to recognise a higher order solution to the problem which resolves the apparent conflict (Mugny, Perret-Clermont and Doise, 1981). For this to occur, it is necessary that the children's initial solutions differ, but it is not necessary for any of them to be more advanced than the others, or for any of them to be correct. The real 'ratchet' driving the process is that resolution of children's partial or centred solutions can in the end only be found by adopting a higher level, more decentred solution, thus ensuring cognitive progress.

Perret-Clermont (1980) used essentially the same three-stage experimental design in a series of experiments on peer facilitation of conservation judgements. Pre-tests were individual, and involved a range of standard Piagetian assessments of children's understanding of conservation of quantity. Various arrangements were tried out for the children assigned to the social interaction condition in the second session. One which proved effective was to assign two 'conservers' and one 'non-conserver' to work together. The non-conserver was then given a task such as sharing out between the children by pouring from a jug into three different shaped glasses. The session went on until all the children agreed that they each had the same quantity. The non-conserving children exposed to this kind of interaction went on to show significant pre- to post-test gains on standard tests of conservation of liquid quantity.

With conservation, as with the village task, progress could result even from interaction between two non-conservers, provided that they generated differing initial judgements. These studies further highlighted the potential benefits of peer interaction for the development of children's thinking, and the supposedly key role of socio-cognitive conflict in underpinning them. They certainly helped to stimulate research interest in this area, and indeed triggered our own initial studies reported later in this chapter. Not surprisingly, however, they also engendered some controversy.

Reservations about socio-cognitive conflict

Doise and colleagues attracted a good deal of attention in the early 1980s, and not a little criticism. Russell (1981, 1982) argued that in tasks such as conservation the pre-operational child was in effect responding with an *opinion* of how the array looked after transformation. By contrast, the operational child was responding in terms of what is objectively the case. The difference, as Russell sees it, is one of 'propositional attitude'. Pre-operational children coming up with differing answers could quite well (and, Russell suggests, often do) simply agree to disagree. If and when conflict is effective, on this argument, it should be by prompting the children towards the adoption of an appropriate objective attitude, allowing them to bring to bear understandings that they already possess.

The idea that young children might in fact understand more about conservation than their responses on standard Piagetian tests would suggest was one of the main themes of Donaldson's influential book *Children's Minds* (1978). McGarrigle and Donaldson, as early as 1975, were able to show that manipulations to the context of presentation of conservation tasks, such as having the transformation of materials appear accidental, could have a dramatic effect upon children's responses. Donaldson suggested that the standard conservation procedure contained misleading socio-communicative cues to the child to attend to appearances, rather than to the actual quantities concerned. The very deliberate way in which the transformation of apparent quantity was effected made this the natural focus for the child's attention. When the transformation occurred as a seemingly accidental consequence of the activities of an errant teddy bear, the child was able to discount the transformation as irrelevant to the actual quantities involved.

Other similar studies followed. In some studies of our own, we were able to show that even where the transformation of materials was deliberately done by the experimenter, children would discount it if some plausible rationale for it was provided. Thus Light, Buckingham and Robbins (1979) used a badly chipped beaker as a reason for pouring the contents from one container to another, which just 'happened' to be of a different shape. This was done in the context of setting up a game for the children, who were tested in pairs. The game was such that it was important for quantities to be equal, but the chip in the beaker would make the game dangerous; thus the need to find another container. A substantial majority of five and six-year-olds judged that the resulting transformation did *not* affect the quantities involved, whereas almost all children of this age fail on the standard version of the same task.

This result has proved replicable (e.g. Miller, 1982), but the interpretation put on it at the time may well be the wrong one. That interpretation stressed the fact that the transformation was made to seem incidental to the proceedings, rather than central to them. Later research using different designs (Roazzi and Bryant, 1992) has failed to find significant effects for such 'incidentality'. On the other hand, our own subsequent studies have shown that setting the conservation task in the context of a *game* is sufficient by itself to improve children's performance.

For example, Light, Gorsuch and Newman (1987) presented pairs of five and six-year-olds with a heap of dried peas for them to divide into two equal heaps. These were then put into two rather differently shaped containers, and the children were asked whether the quantities remained equal. For some of them, all this was done in the context of setting up a game in which they were going to compete with one another to move their peas as fast as they could to a target container, using a straw. The children who encountered the conservation questions in this context were much more likely to respond correctly than those who encountered the same transformation and the same questions without the game setting. So it seems that when children are working in pairs and anticipating a competitive game, they construe the conservation test procedures differently. In this situation they remain resolutely attentive to the quantities involved, and are not readily distracted by the appearances.

Things are actually rather more complicated. It can be argued (Light, 1986) that in these modified versions of the conservation test the children are really just complying with the apparent wishes and expectations of the experimenter. Just as the standard versions of these tasks might lead children toward the wrong response, these versions may in various ways cue the correct response, even in children with no firm grasp of conservation. Indeed we have been able to show that similar modifications can elicit 'conserving' responses even in situations where the quantity in question is not in fact conserved (Light and Gilmour, 1983).

For present purposes, however, this is not really important. What is important is that serious question marks were appearing about the validity of these kinds of Piagetian tests, and the stability of children's responses to them. More particularly, there are clear suggestions from this literature that children in pairs or small groups may well interpret given tasks and questions differently from the way in which the same tasks and questions would be understood by individuals. Improvements in performance, at the time and subsequently, may reflect this altered understanding of the questions at least as much as it reflects any socio-cognitive conflict arising from different points of view within the group.

One thing that makes this alternative point of view attractive is that peer facilitation processes sometimes seem to work just *too* well. Thus, for example, Perret-Clermont (1980) found that social class differences in children's pre-test performance on conservation tasks were typically large, but after a session of interaction of the kind described earlier, the differences according to class disappeared. Similar findings have been reported for urban–rural differences, and ethnic differences (Light and Perret-Clermont, 1991).

If the pre-test differences were genuinely reflective of differences in the children's levels of achievement in this crucial area of cognitive development, is it really conceivable that such differences could be wiped out by a single session of ten to fifteen minutes of interaction? It seems much more plausible that the initial differences reflect differences in children's understanding of the meaning and reference of the conservation questions, and indeed there is some independent evidence that this is the case (Grossen, 1988).

It would seem that what disambiguates the questions for the children is the experience of sharing in the paired or group session, leading Light and Perret-Clermont to conclude that: 'the efficacy of the peer interaction procedure arises not (or not only) from the socio-cognitive conflict mechanism . . . but from the introduction of a norm of equality which serves to support correct responses, which are then carried over to the individual post-test' (1991, p.145).

This issue of how social norms influence cognitive functioning surfaced in a number of areas of research in the 1980s, not least in Doise's own work on the influence of 'social marking'. However, we shall leave the further exploration of this issue for a later chapter. In the remaining sections of this chapter, we shall turn from Piaget to Vygotsky to find a rather different set of 'starting points' for research on social (and more particularly peer) processes in learning.

Learning as the co-construction of understanding

Vygotsky's writings of the 1920s and 1930s, though they led to a robust tradition of research in the Soviet Union, had little real impact on Western developmental psychology for nearly half a century. In the 1980s, however, there was a rush of translation, commentary and exploitation of

'Vygotskian' approaches in relation to a whole range of research problems (e.g. Bruner, 1985; Wertsch, 1985; Newman, Griffin and Cole, 1989; Forman, Minick and Stone, 1993).

Vygotsky's work has perhaps contributed to this field in two main ways. The first rests on his attempts to characterise the fine-grained interpersonal interactions that take place in learning settings, and involves concepts such as the 'zone of proximal development' and 'scaffolding'. The second rests on his broader attempt to develop a 'cultural psychology', within which learning is seen to depend upon mediation by social, cultural and institutional processes at many levels. We shall explore both of these contributions.

Vygotsky was interested in the origins of what he termed the higher mental functions: thinking, reasoning and understanding. The development of these higher mental functions in humans was seen as a fundamentally social rather than individual process. The child's interactions with other people serve to mediate between the child and the world-to-be-learned-about, and so understanding learning depends upon understanding the particular types of interactions which serve to foster it.

The concept of a zone of proximal development is central to this approach. Children, or indeed adults, can be characterised in terms of what they can achieve unaided. Indeed most forms of assessment involve testing what individuals can do without help. But individuals may also differ in terms of what they can do *with* help. The attainments which are possible for an individual given a measure of support and guidance are, as Vygotsky put it, within that individual's zone of proximal development (ZPD). They are attainments that will be possible for that individual unaided at some point in the near future.

The concept of a ZPD is thus an integral part of a theory of teaching and learning. Tharp and Gallimore (1988) have elaborated this aspect of Vygotsky's work into what they call a theory of teaching as assisted performance. They see learning as a process of guided re-invention, whereby social guidance makes it possible for the learner to achieve a constructive intellectual 're-invention' of some piece of culturally elaborated knowledge. The emphasis upon understanding being a matter of construction is clearly shared with Piagetian approaches. The distinctive features are (i) recognition that much of what the learner needs to learn is already in some sense 'available' in the culture, and (ii) recognition that interpersonal processes play a key role in making that culturally elaborated learning available to the individual.

Not unnaturally, given this emphasis on guidance, Vygotsky saw the relevant interpersonal interactions as going on between the learner and a more capable 'other'. Indeed, he defined the ZPD as: 'The distance between the actual developmental level as determined by individual problem solving and the level of potential development as determined through problem solving under adult guidance *or in collaboration with more capable peers*' (Vygotsky, 1978, p. 86, our emphasis). As with Piaget, then, peer interaction is flagged as having a potentially important role in learning and development. But whereas Piaget's emphasis was on the status-symmetry of such interactions, Vygotsky's emphasis is more on the competence-*a*symmetry that will often be a feature of peer relations. As Tharp and Gallimore put it, to the extent that peers can assist performance, learning will occur through their assistance.

The concept which has been most widely used to capture the forms of guidance which support learners in their progress through the ZPD is that of 'scaffolding'. Introduced by Wood, Bruner and Ross (1976), it captures the sense in which, through encouragement, focusing, demonstrations, reminders and suggestions, a learner can be supported in mastering a task or achieving an understanding. To take the building analogy further, if we imagine building an arch with bricks it is easy to see the vital role played by the wooden 'formwork' used to assemble the arch. However, the role of this scaffolding is strictly temporary; when complete the arch will hold itself up, though without scaffolding it could not have been built.

Tharp and Gallimore see progression through the ZPD in terms of four stages. In the first, performance is directly assisted by more capable others through 'scaffolding' of one kind or another. In the second, the learner effectively takes over the role of the 'scaffolder' in relation to his or her own learning. This often means 'talking oneself through' a task, remembering requests, reminders and injunctions previously given, and so on. The third stage is marked by the falling away of such 'self-guidance', as performance becomes automatic. The fourth 'stage' just recognises the fact that we can get thrown back to earlier stages of the acquisition process by such stressors as tiredness, or by changes in the precise conditions of the task. Learning to drive provides a useful case in point for all of these stages of learning.

It is as a model of adult guidance of children's learning that most direct use has been made of these concepts. For example, Wood and colleagues (see Wood, 1986) conducted a series of investigations of how four-year-old children can be taught to assemble a 3D puzzle involving wooden blocks and pegs. First they observed mothers' attempts to teach their own children how to complete the puzzle. The mothers who succeeded best were those who shifted their levels of intervention flexibly according to how well the child was doing. This 'contingency strategy' can be seen as a way for the mother to gauge and monitor the child's ZPD as learning proceeds, and to provide scaffolding at just the right point.

In further studies Wood and colleagues showed that the adoption of a 'contingent' strategy by specially trained tutors also resulted in better learning outcomes than any of the alternatives explored. In their recent work (Wood and Wood, 1996, in press), they have been working towards the development of computer-based tutoring systems which will provide optimally contingent patterns of tutorial support; something which human tutors, even given training, find it extremely difficult to do.

Although Wood and colleagues are intent on improving upon 'what comes naturally', much of the research done from a Vygotskian standpoint has tended to see effective teaching and learning exchanges as essentially incidental to ongoing joint engagement in activities, whether between mothers and children in the home (e.g. Rogoff and Gardner, 1984; Rogoff, 1990) or between experts and novices in traditional craft practices such as tailoring or weaving (Greenfield and Lave, 1982; Lave and Wenger, 1991).

Attempts have been made, however, to use a Vygotskian approach to illuminate what is going on in the classroom. Perhaps the most successful is that of Edwards and Mercer (1987), who explored how, by skillfully guiding classroom discussion, the class teacher can establish and maintain a focus of shared attention, provide children with a language in which to describe their own experiences and, using that language, build up a body of 'common knowledge' about the topic in hand. On the other hand, attempts to apply the concept of scaffolding more directly in relation to classroom practice have in at least some cases (e.g. Bliss, Askew and Macrae 1996) been unable to find any evidence for such processes at all.

Vygotsky's ideas about the social-interactional bases of learning have also inspired a considerable number of studies of learning in the context of peer interaction. As one might expect, a good proportion of these involve interactions in which an older, more experienced or pre-trained individual is designated as tutor to a younger, less experienced or untrained peer. This kind of 'peer tutoring' has been shown to be effective both in experimental studies (e.g. Phelps and Damon, 1989) and in applied educational contexts (e.g. Topping, 1994). It may indeed have benefits for the peer tutors as well as the peer tutees (Barron and Foot, 1991).

As Hogan and Tudge (in press) note, there has been relatively little research on peer collaboration, as opposed to peer tutoring, approached from a Vygotskian standpoint. However, increasingly since the mid 1980s, Vygotskian ideas have come to colour the interpretations offered by researchers for peer facilitation effects observed in experimental studies.

For example, Forman and Cazden (1985) studied joint problem solving by pairs of nine- to fourteen-year-olds. Their problem-solving tasks included Piaget's chemical combinations task (Inhelder and Piaget, 1958) and a task involving predicting the shape of the shadows of various objects, when lit from various positions. Their observations of exchanges between the children highlighted the importance of well coordinated joint activity in, for example, setting up the apparatus and planning the experiments. Establishing shared goals and building a shared understanding of the task are just the kinds of 'co-constructive' activities that a Vygotskian analysis might lead one to look for in effective peer interaction. On the other hand, in the interpretation of the results of the experiments, Forman and Cazden saw clear indications that differences of interpretation, defended and argued over, could be productive in much the way that a Piagetian analysis would lead one to expect.

Both theoretical approaches may thus have something to offer, in drawing attention to different aspects of productive interaction. While a Piagetian approach highlights what being confronted with a socio-cognitive conflict can do for individual cognitive development, a Vygotskian approach highlights the way in which a shared understanding can be arrived at through a process which might be termed 'mutual construction'. We shall return to this issue in more detail in subsequent chapters, but here we want to turn to a rather wider reading of what Vygotsky might have to offer to an understanding of social processes in learning.

A socio-cultural approach to learning

The study of social processes in learning can lead into polarised arguments about 'which comes first, the individual or the social/cultural setting?'. Vygotsky attempted to avoid either kind of reduction by focusing on 'mediated action', adopting a broad theoretical approach to development which is nowadays usually referred to as a socio-cultural approach.

Wertsch (1997, 1998) summarises the properties of mediated action in the following terms. Mediated action involves a relationship between an agent and a 'mediational means' or a 'cultural tool'. Wertsch uses the example of pole vaulting: both the pole (a culturally given tool) and the pole vaulter are intrinsic to the activity. A more cognitive example might be the use of a word-processing or drawing package on a computer; the cultural tool both lends itself to being used in various kinds of ways and at the same time imposes various kinds of constraints.

The notion of cultural tools extends to symbolic tools elaborated within a culture, so that a mathematical algorithm which allows you to do mental arithmetic is just as much a cultural tool as is a pocket calculator. Language itself (or at least any particular language, elaborated for any particular set of purposes) can be considered as a cultural tool. Thus virtually all intelligent activity involves interacting with a range of cultural tools, and competence in the use of such tools is central both to intellectual development and to becoming an effective member of society.

To return to Wertsch's example of the pole vaulter, the advent of a new type of pole can make new records possible. Probably some pole vaulters will adopt the new type of pole with enthusiasm and 'make it their own', while others will stick resolutely with the old technology. This sense of 'making something your own' is often referred to as 'appropriation', and catches at the sense in which cultural tools are not just picked up and put down as and when needed. Rather they become part of how we construe the world, how we approach problems and even how we relate to one another.

The appropriation of cultural tools involves more than simply having access to them. Cultural tools in general are associated in complex ways with the distribution of power and authority within the culture. In the case of computers, for example, powerful vested interests shape the resources which become available to individuals, and issues of access and equity arise very pointedly (Light, 1997; Littleton, 1995, 1996).

A socio-cultural approach thus directs us not only to look at the potentialities of collaborative interactions for learning in a particular way, but also to relate the interactional processes observed to the institutional contexts in which such collaborative interactions occur. This consideration will come to be a salient one in relation to some of the issues such as gender which will occupy us in later chapters in this volume.

Piaget and Vygotsky: complementary constructions of collaboration

What becomes evident from this review of Piagetian and Vygotskian approaches is that they have many features in common which differentiate them from learning theory traditions. For both, learning is a matter of active construction, the ingredients for which are to be found in the physical and social world. Vygotsky's stress on the mediated character of action extends Piaget's account in ways which add to its reach in important respects, while not quarrelling with its basic tenets. Between them, these two approaches to understanding development and learning have shaped almost all of the research to be described and discussed in this volume. We shall have occasion to reflect at various points on how well these perspectives have served their purpose in framing this field of research.

In the next chapter, though, we shall move rather sharply from the general to the particular, by giving a synopsis of the series of experimental studies which represent our own first attempts to come to grips with the phenomena of collaborative learning.

2   Peers and puzzles: a first series of studies

Introduction

Our own interest in conducting empirical research on peer interaction as a facilitator of children's problem solving was raised mainly by exposure to the neo-Piagetian research of Doise and colleagues, described in the previous chapter. However, the doubts raised earlier about the validity of Piagetian procedures for assessing conservation were also being raised by our own and others' research in relation to a wide range of other Piagetian tests. These included the spatial perspective taking tasks which had been so extensively used by Doise and colleagues in their peer interaction studies (Donaldson, 1978; Light and Nix, 1983).

Since our interest was the more general question of when, if at all, 'two heads are better than one', it seemed sensible to move beyond the particular case of children's mastery of 'concrete operational reasoning' to consider a wider range of ages and types of task. Nonetheless, as will be apparent from the account which follows, the basic three-stage experimental design which had been adopted by Doise and others was carried over fairly intact into these studies.

The first Tower of Hanoi study

The Tower of Hanoi is a traditional game which has not infrequently been used by cognitive psychologists to study problem solving. A typical version is shown in Figure 2.1. Here the materials consist of a baseboard with three vertical pegs, and a number of 'tiles'. These each have a hole in and can be placed on any of the pegs (the little handles on the tiles are an adaptation for our particular purposes). Figure 2.1 shows a possible initial position, with all the tiles being stacked in order of size on peg (A). The object, on any particular occasion, might be to move all the tiles to peg (C), so that they end up similarly ordered by size on that peg. The constraints are that only one tile may be removed from a peg at a time, and at no point can a larger tile be placed on top of a smaller one. If three

14

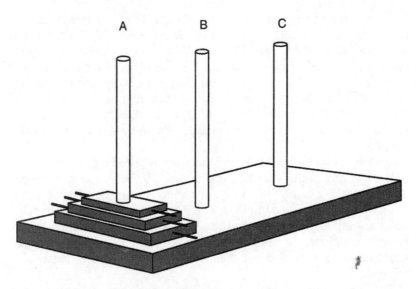

Figure 2.1 The Tower of Hanoi

tiles are to be moved, as in Figure 2.1, then the player has to move the smallest to (C), the middle tile to (B), the smallest to (B), the largest to (C), the smallest to (A), the middle tile to (C) and finally the smallest to (C), a total of seven moves. The solution path thus involves a series of 'detours', which form nested subroutines.

We conducted two experiments with this task (Glachan and Light, 1982; Light and Glachan, 1985) using a version very like that shown in Figure 2.1. In essence, we simply wanted to know whether two children, performing the task together over a series of trials, would learn how to do it better than a single child would. As far as the children's learning outcomes were concerned, would 'two heads be better than one'?

Our first study was conducted with twenty-eight eight-year-olds. All were given a first session with the task (a 'pre-test') on their own, in which they completed three trials with two-tile towers (which are very easy) and then three trials with three-tile towers. Their pre-test scores were based on the three-tile trials, all of which began with the tiles on one of the outer pegs.

Two weeks later, the children all had a second session, which we can call the practice session. This time twelve were assigned (at random) to work alone, while the remaining sixteen children worked in eight pairs, again with assignment being random except that all were same-sex pairs.

On this occasion they had eight trials on the Tower of Hanoi, all with three tiles and all beginning on the centre peg, with the 'goal' peg alternating from trial to trial. They were told to try to solve the problem in the fewest possible moves, and that the minimum possible number of moves was seven. The children working in pairs sat opposite one another, at opposite sides of the puzzle. They were told that tile moving must be done by both of them together, one holding each handle. A week later, all children had a final post-test session which was individual and identical to the pre-test.

Analysis of strategies for solving the task suggested a number of more or less efficient strategies, taking seven, nine, eleven and thirteen moves. Solutions taking eight, ten, twelve and fourteen moves reflected use of one of these strategies combined with a corrected error at some point. Solutions taking more than fourteen moves all seemed to contain haphazard sequences of moves, and were treated as 'non-strategic'. Children were classified by their predominant solution patterns at pre-test.

The study revealed that there was significantly greater improvement from pre-test to post-test for those children who had been paired for the practice session than for those who had worked alone. Closer analysis indicated that this differential benefit from working in pairs applied only to those children who showed some sort of strategic approach to the problem at the pre-test stage. Since children were assigned to pairs at random, most of the pairs comprised children with differing pre-test performances. We looked at those children who had been the 'better' member of their pair, in terms of pre-test performance, and matched them up with children from the individual condition with similar pre-test performance. Those who had worked in pairs still showed significantly greater pre- to post-test improvement, indicating that in at least some circumstances the experience of working in pairs can be advantageous even if one's partner is less able than oneself.

The second Tower of Hanoi study

A second study replicated the same sequence of sessions as the first, but in this case all children were paired in the second session. Eighty children took part, again eight year olds. With all allocations being random, within sex, some of the children worked under the same instructions as before ('structured interaction'), for others the requirement to move each tile together, using the handles, was not introduced ('unstructured interaction'). For the remainder, an adult coached the pairs in the correct seven move solution ('instruction').

This time, pre- and post-test trials included both the 'centre-peg start' trials used in the second session and the 'end-peg start' trials used in the previous pre- and post-tests. All types of second session were equally effective in terms of producing good post-test performances on the 'centre-peg start' trials actually used in the second session. However, the structured interaction condition was significantly superior to the other conditions as regards pre- to post-test improvement on the 'end-peg start' trials. In fact it seemed that only children in the structured interaction condition were able to extend what they had learned to related problems.

These results lend themselves quite well to interpretation in terms of the productive potential of cognitive conflict. The fact that children lacking any strategic approach to the task were relatively unaffected by the various manipulations is consistent with the idea that one has to have a viewpoint of one's own in order to experience a conflict between this viewpoint and that of a partner. In order to experience conflict, children must be pursuing some kind of plan or strategy of their own.

The ineffectiveness of direct coaching (which was done by modelling solutions rather than by explanations) in producing generalised improvement may be seen in terms of the children's lack of opportunity to experiment and resolve conflicts between the modelled solution and their own previous strategy.

The superiority of the 'structured' over the 'unstructured' interaction condition is illuminated by the observation (from videotape analysis) that while both children appeared to be genuinely engaged in all moves in the structured condition, almost 90 per cent of moves in the unstructured condition appeared to be determined and carried out entirely by one child. There was little discussion and almost no indication of joint decision making. Moreover, many of these pairs were marked by a high degree of dominance. In the majority of the unstructured pairs, one of the children determined at least twice as many moves as the other. In this situation the dominant individual would have experienced little conflict, while the submissive individual would have little opportunity to resolve any conflict experienced.

These first two studies, then, attest to the potential value of peer interaction in problem solving, using a task remote from the Piagetian repertoire. They indicated that the productivity of this form of interaction depends on the parties to the interaction having definite ideas of their own about how to approach the task, and having an opportunity to express these. They make clear that the presentation of a correct solution to the problem is neither a necessary nor a sufficient condition to produce progress. Under some circumstances at least, it seemed, two wrongs could indeed make a right.

The third Tower of Hanoi study

A further study, conducted with a very different version of the Tower of Hanoi task, allowed us some further insights into the conditions under which collaborative problem solving with this task could be productive of good learning outcomes for children (Light, Foot, Colbourn and McClelland, 1987). For this study, we employed a computer-based version of the task, the screen presentation for which is shown in Figure 2.2. The object and the rules remain the same, but now making a 'move' involves keying in a number to indicate the position from which a disc is to be removed and then another number to indicate where it should be placed.

One of the attractions of this version of the task is that it allows automatic collection of move sequence data, and of course it also allows illegal moves to be prevented automatically. However, unless supplementary constraints are built in, it does not 'force' the children's joint engagement in each move. In a replication and extension of the previous study, we attempted to compare the effectiveness of paired interaction around this version of the problem with and without such supplementary constraints.

Sixty children between eight and nine years of age participated in this study. All were pre-tested individually on the task. After a brief demonstration they had two trials, both with three 'tiles', moving from position 1 to 2 and then from 2 to 3. On the second session, a week later, the children were given the same two trials, three times each, each time trying to complete the task in the smallest possible number of moves. Following random assignment, twenty children worked individually and twenty worked in pairs under instructions to work out each move together and to agree it before moving anything. This condition was referred to as 'unstructured interaction'.

The remaining twenty children were assigned to a 'structured interaction' condition in which the same general instructions were given, but in addition the keyboard was constrained so as to accept instructions only when they were keyed in simultaneously from two separate keypads (one 'belonging' to each child), specially labelled up at opposite ends of the keyboard. Thus the children were effectively forced to agree the entry, and both of them had to be involved in the execution of each move. This reproduces the same type of constraint represented by the requirement that each child hold the handles on the tiles in the physical version of the task.

Individual post-tests included the two trials that the children had worked on previously, together with two further trials, involving moving from position 3 to 1, and from 2 to 1. In terms of performance on the

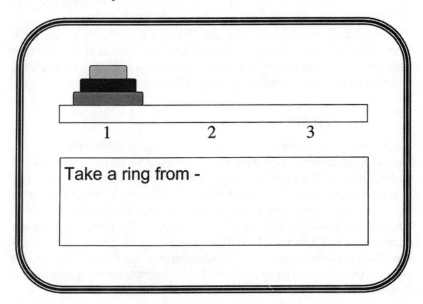

Take a ring from -

Figure 2.2 The computer version of the Tower of Hanoi

practice session (session two), the pairs did rather better than the individuals, with nothing to choose between the two types of pairing. However, at post-test, fully correct (seven move) solutions were significantly and substantially more frequent in the structured condition than in either of the others, though only for the trials which reproduced the moves practised in the earlier sessions.

It seems, then, that what the children are effectively learning in the structured condition is not a generalised solution strategy, but rather a particular sequence of moves. Nonetheless, the fact that only the structured condition led to any detectable superiority over individual practice confirms the indications from the previous study that it is not simply exposure to solutions that differ from your own, but actually being forced to engage with them in some way, which fosters improved performance.

Children working collaboratively on the Tower of Hanoi task, whether using the 'physical' or the computer version, did not typically talk to one another very much. This is of some interest in that it suggests that talk is not the 'be all and end all' of collaborative learning, an issue to which we shall return in later chapters. But at the time we saw the dearth of task-related talk as a drawback, inasmuch as it made it difficult to examine relationships between the quality of interaction in a particular pair and the progress made by the members of that pair. Talk is relatively easy to 'collect', and more amenable to analysis than non-verbal aspects of interaction. For this reason, amongst others, we extended our research programme to a rather different type of problem, namely a code-breaking problem based on the pegboard game 'Mastermind'.

The first Mastermind study

A version of the 'Mastermind' game was available commercially in the form of a microchip-based device called 'Logic 5', and this was used in our first study of this problem. The device selected a three-digit sequence at random, and the task was to determine this sequence by entering three-digit sequences via a keypad and getting feedback via a visual display. The feedback informed the player(s) of the number of correct digits and the number of these that were in the correct position. Pilot work suggested that this was something children of a range of ages would be interested in and that, when pairs of children were working together on it, it would elicit a good deal of task-related talk.

We worked with children of two age levels for this study; a class of seven year olds and a class of twelve to thirteen year olds, sixty-four children in all. The initial individual session was more of a training session than a pre-test. The task was explained to the children, with particular care being taken to make sure that they understood the meaning of the feedback.

The children were shown how to record each of their proposed sequences on a paper and pencil record pad before entering it. Then, they had two practice turns on the task, being allowed up to twenty 'guesses' to break each code. However, since the generated code sequences were genuinely random, and some were considerably harder to 'break' than others, this introduction did not provide a reliable pre-test score for each child.

Within each of the age levels, children were then allocated at random to either an individual condition or a single-sex pair condition for the second session. In this session they were allowed forty 'entries', with which they had to solve as many problems as possible. Those working in pairs were told that they had to work together, to agree each entry before recording it on the sheet, and then take turns in actually keying in the numbers. Video-recordings were made of the paired sessions. A week later all the children were given an individual post-test session where they were given four problems to solve in a maximum of twenty entries each.

The results showed a significant advantage at post-test for those children who had worked in pairs at stage two. These children required a mean of 8 entries in the case of the older children and 11 entries in the case of the younger children to solve each problem. Those who had worked alone throughout required 11 and 15 entries respectively. Thus the seven year olds who had worked in pairs were as good at the task at post-test as the twelve- to thirteen-year-olds who had worked on their own.

There were also promising indications from the transcribed video-recordings that the nature and extent of the talk that went on between the children in the paired sessions was correlated with these children's post-test performances. However, the lack of any adequate measure of pre-test performance in this study meant that it was not possible to establish a causal relationship; it might simply have been a reflection of children with a better grasp of the task talking more. An adequate pre-test required us to be able to specify simpler, introductory two-digit 'code' sequences, and then to control the sequences selected to ensure comparability across participants. We achieved these aims by creating our own microcomputer-based version of the task for a second study.

The second Mastermind study

This study involved seven and eight year olds, forty in all. All were pre-tested individually using two-digit sequences to introduce the task and three standard three-digit sequences to get a pre-test score. All children were then allocated randomly to same-sex pairs for a second session, which was run just as in the previous study. Finally, all children had an individual post-test similar to the pre-test (Light and Glachan, 1985).

Videotapes of the second, paired, session were used as a basis for categorising the pairs into 'high argumentation' and 'low argumentation' pairs. An argument, for these purposes, referred to an identifiable difference of opinion resolved by some form of explanation or justification related to the problem. Such arguments in many cases included several verbal 'counters', along with explanations, inferences, and so on. As it transpired, ten of the pairs fell into a high argumentation group, with more than ten such arguments, while the other ten low argumentation pairs all had means of fewer than five arguments.

The high argumentation and low argumentation pairs turned out not to differ in terms of the pre-test scores of the children concerned. Indeed, the pre-test scores of those who ended up in the low argumentation pairs were very slightly better. However, the individual post-tests results showed better performance from the children who had been in high argumentation pairings, and an analysis of variance showed a significant interaction between pre- to post-test improvement and the level of argumentation.

Looking more closely at the arguments themselves, it appeared that what was important was that the children remained focused on the content of the problem and attempted to resolve their disagreement through argument. It was relatively unimportant, it seemed, whether the agreed outcome was the more appropriate of the alternatives under consideration. The low argumentation pairings were characterised by a tendency to simply assert a judgement as to what to do next, and if possible to disregard the partner and press ahead. In the end either one partner took over completely or turn-taking rules were invoked by the partners.

These results were based upon a very crude typology of verbal argument, but they do suggest that, with a verbal task such as Mastermind, aspects of the verbal interaction may give clear pointers to what it is that is productive about the experience of working in pairs or small groups. This is an issue which will be explored in a good deal more depth in the following chapters. Meanwhile there is one more strand of research to be detailed here, involving a more familiar task, namely the balance beam.

Two balance beam studies

The stages through which children typically progress in achieving an understanding of how weight and distance influence the balancing of a beam on a fulcrum have long been studied by psychologists (Inhelder and Piaget, 1958; Siegler, 1976). Since the problem is one in which the interrelations of several relevant factors need to be taken into account to achieve a correct understanding, it offered an attractive candidate for a study of collaborative problem solving. We conducted several studies using a computer version of a balance beam task, the basic screen presentation of which is shown in Figure 2.3. On each trial, a beam is presented with weights already in position, and the task is to predict whether such a beam would tip, and if so, which way.

The first study using this task was conducted with eighty twelve-year-old children (Light and Foot, 1987). It involved an individual pre-test for all children using a paper and pencil version of the task, predicting which way a series of beams would tip. At stage two the computer version was used. Half of the children worked individually, while the others worked in pairs. All of the pairs were asked to work together, but half of them had the additional requirement that they had to come up with an agreed reason for their prediction before keying it in. Half of the children working individually were also asked to come up with a reason for their judgements before keying them in. The experimenter was on hand as 'audience' to the

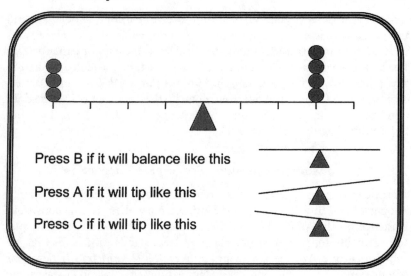

Figure 2.3 The balance beam task

children's justifications, but these were always received without comment. All children were subsequently individually post-tested.

In terms of pre to post-test improvement, the individual condition worked least well, and adding the requirement for justifications had no significant beneficial effect. The paired condition without justifications was not significantly better than the individual conditions, but the paired condition *with* the requirement for justifications did produce significantly better post-test performance than either of the individual conditions. It turned out on closer inspection that although the children in the 'pairs plus justification' condition were doing better than the others, the strategy which most of them were using involved adding rather than multiplying the effects of weight and distance. Although this strategy is not correct, its systematic use in this case resulted in a fairly high proportion of correct predictions.

Partly as a way of distinguishing strategies, and partly for the purposes of replication, a second study was conducted using a variant of the previous task. Here, a beam was presented with weights at given positions to one side of the fulcrum only. The task was to place weights to the other side of the fulcrum in such a way as to balance the beam. The direct mirroring of the weights and positions on the two sides was not allowed, and the software would not execute it, so the children had to find an alternative solution.

Once again, eighty children of around twelve years of age took part, and the conditions were just the same as in the previous study. The results showed even more clearly than in the previous study that neither pairing nor justification had much impact on their own, but when combined in the 'pairs plus justification' condition the result was significantly better. Average pre- to post-test improvement in the 'pairs plus justification' condition was in fact more than twice as great as for any of the other conditions (Light and Foot, 1987).

Friendship and productivity in peer interaction

Despite frequent suggestions that friendship pairs should find it easier to cooperate and thus benefit from peer interaction, there is little consistent evidence on this point. Berndt, Perry and Miller (1988), for example, found no difference in the gains made by friends and non-friends working together, while Azmitia and Montgomery (1993) did find benefits for 'friendship pairs' as compared with 'acquaintance pairs' on at least some of the scientific reasoning tasks studied.

This variable was addressed in one of our own smaller studies (Light, Foot, Colbourn and McClelland, 1987). Eleven year olds were asked to nominate the three classmates with whom they most liked to work (note that this is not quite the same thing as friendship, but undoubtedly covaries with it strongly). The children were assigned to same sex groups of three. Four of these groups (referred to as mutually nominating groups) included only children who had nominated both their partners, while the other four groups included no partner nominations. The groups were matched for gender and for general cognitive abilities, using the results of a school test recently administered to all the children.

The groups of children were given worksheet geography problems which they had to answer using a computer database. They were encouraged to work collaboratively, and were given three twenty-minute sessions on successive days to work on the task. Video-recordings of interactions in the groups were scored (at the level of individuals) for such behaviours as ignoring, agreeing with or disagreeing with a proposal, and reference to the worksheet. None of these measures indicated a significant difference between the mutually nominating groups and the others.

The mutually nominating groups sought less help from the experimenter/teacher, and related to this was the finding that these groups made significantly fewer keyboard errors. There was no indication of difference in terms of the children's grasp of the fundamentals of the task, but the relatively low level of minor 'glitches' in the mutually nominating groups did seem indicative of more effective mutual support, or perhaps lower anxiety. There were no significant differences in terms of expressed attitudes towards the task at the end of the study.

Overview

As will be apparent, the studies described in this chapter involved a fairly arbitrary choice of tasks. Most were tasks which had been used by other students of problem solving, and were essentially intellectual rather than sensorimotor problems. The Tower of Hanoi task demanded forward planning, while Mastermind required a systematic use of feedback and a recognition of the significance of negative evidence. The balance beam comes nearest to the kinds of Piagetian task discussed earlier in this chapter, in that it demands an ability to recognise and coordinate the contributions of two discrete variables to the behaviour of the beam.

If the tasks were more heterogeneous than in much previous work, so too was the age range. The children involved in these studies ranged from seven to thirteen years of age, but there was little indication that this in itself was a significant factor in shaping the results. The tight tie between the mechanism of peer facilitation and a particular phase of intellectual development, suggested by the socio-cognitive conflict theory, sits rather uneasily with our results. It seems rather that whatever processes are involved operate in a rather similar fashion across a considerable range both of tasks and age levels.

Broadly, the findings of these studies do seem to confirm that the pairing of children while they work on a problem can improve their performance on similar problems when they meet them on their own at a later date. The first Tower of Hanoi study showed that such facilitation can occur even for the initially more able member of a pair of children, but is likely to occur only for children who from the outset have at least some ideas of their own about how to tackle the problem. The second Tower of Hanoi study indicated that the benefits of peer interaction depended on keeping the children jointly engaged and preventing dominance and 'turn-taking'. The third Tower of Hanoi study confirmed this finding in relation to a computer-based version of the task, though the gains here were limited to the specific trials used in the paired session.

The Tower of Hanoi studies were characterised by very low levels of task-related talk between the members even of the most effective pairs. By contrast, Mastermind elicited high levels of discussion, and, in some pairings, high levels of disagreement about what entries to make and why. The level of such argument turned out to be associated quite clearly with the pre- to post-test gains made by the members of such pairs. Similarly, the balance beam task lent itself to verbal justification of the proposed solutions, and the two studies reported here both suggest that it was the combination of the availability of a partner and the requirement for such justification which resulted in the highest levels of progress. The fact that the verbal articulation of a justification was not in itself sufficient to produce such progress suggests that it is the process of agreeing a justification that holds the key to the productivity of this condition. Reconciling disagreements might of course be a part of this process.

Thus, the findings reported here are consistent with the idea of productive conflict of views between partners, but the conception of conflict required is rather broader than Doise's original socio-cognitive conflict hypothesis seemed to suggest. The presence of differing points of view may be a necessary ingredient of productive conflict, in this sense, but so too may be a means of securing and sustaining the joint engagement of all the parties in the resolution of disagreements. The focus on verbal interaction and on the co-construction of solutions to tasks, more characteristic of Vygotskian approaches, also finds some support in these studies.

Of course, the series of studies revisited here represent only one of many possible approaches to the empirical study of peer interaction of children's learning, and are subject to many limitations. The studies were conducted in school, but not in the context of ongoing classroom activity, nor by the regular classroom teacher. For the most part they involved random allocation of children to experimental conditions, thus riding roughshod over such considerations as friendship patterns. The final study suggested that this was not an irrelevant consideration.

Most of the studies described also focused not on pair or group performance as such, but on individual pre- to post-test performance changes. These were used as a measure of facilitation of individual learning as a result of typically single and rather brief periods of paired interaction around a well-defined task.

We shall trace the further development of this line of research work in Chapter 4, but meanwhile in the following chapter we shall turn to look at a specific context for learning, namely learning with computers. The studies described above already reflect a movement towards task presentation using computers, which has a variety of practical advantages for the researcher. By the late 1980s, it became apparent that computers were going to figure prominently in the learning experiences of both children and adults, and researchers began to show considerable interest in the special characteristics and possibilities of this kind of learning. This interest has shaped the direction of subsequent research on social processes in learning to a considerable degree, so a brief review of the 'computers and learning' literature seems appropriate at this juncture.

3   Computers and learning

Introduction

A comprehensive review of the research literature on what computers might have to offer for learning would have to go back a long way to find its starting points (e.g. Suppes, 1966; see also Light, 1997). However, at least in the in the UK, it is only relatively recently that children have been able to secure reliable access to at least one classroom computer, most teachers have received some training in the use of computers, and the school curriculum envisages computer use in most subject areas (Crook, 1994). The prominence given to computers, and the substantial investment of resources entailed in their use, are widespread features of education across the developed world. The psychological theories of learning which have informed the development of educational computer use over the last thirty years or so offer a fair reflection of the psychology of learning more generally across this period. In this chapter we shall explore some of the ways in which psychological accounts of children's learning have contributed to, and been reflected in, the way computer-based learning has developed.

Computers and instruction

Much of the software used in schools, often referred to under the heading of computer-assisted instruction (CAI), owes its origins at least in part to the associationist learning theory tradition in psychology. A leading exponent of that tradition, B.F. Skinner (e.g. 1965), was heavily committed to the idea that machines could be developed which would teach children more effectively than the classroom teacher was able to do. The 'teaching machines' of the 1950s and 1960s were largely unsuccessful, but the development of the microcomputer offered a new lease of life to this idea.

A traditional learning-theory approach involves focusing very narrowly upon achieving some desired pattern of overt behaviour. The generation of desired behaviour patterns is seen in terms of progressive shaping

27

through small incremental steps. The principal mechanism for achieving such shaping is envisaged as being the reinforcement of correct responses through the reliable delivery of rewards.

In contemporary CAI, the idea is that the computer assists the teacher to achieve a specific instructional goal. The classroom teacher cannot give the level of attention to the individual learner that would be required to implement an individualised instructional programme, but the computer can. With CAI, pupils can receive instruction tailored to their individual level, and their own pace of learning. Much of the relevant software offers 'drill and practice' on well-defined skills in areas such as arithmetic and spelling. The 'reinforcement' for success usually relates to some game-like activity which runs in parallel to the routine tasks, but depends on success in them. The tasks typically consist of numerous fixed format items graded in difficulty, with progression depending on correct responses.

This general approach dominated early use of computers in schools, and software in this tradition is probably still more widely used than anything else, at least for children under about nine years of age (Crook, 1994). It is not easy to evaluate the effectiveness of such software, since comparative studies necessarily involve comparison of particular pieces of software with particular alternative ways of teaching the same material. Nonetheless, the available reviews and meta-analyses suggest moderate but worthwhile gains for CAI-taught pupils as compared with 'chalk-and-talk' alternatives (e.g. Niemiec and Walberg, 1987).

Whereas Skinner saw reinforcement of correct responses as the key to progress, contemporary CAI software usually offers some corrective guidance, which depends on the nature of the error made. With most CAI software, however, the level of 'error diagnosis' undertaken by the computer is minimal. More sophisticated versions of such tutorial software attempt to take account of the pattern of errors made by the child, thus modelling the child's reasoning. A model of the learner's current understanding can then in principle be used to select the most appropriate further tasks or instructions. Such an 'intelligent tutoring system' is thus effectively learning about the learner in order to teach.

Intelligent tutoring systems developed to date, however, typically rest on the assumption that the learner's knowledge consists of a subset of adult knowledge, or that the learner is using one of a pre-determined list of erroneous rules (Costa, 1991). Even in the limited areas in which adequate psychological models of children's learning are available, it is not as yet established that in practice an intelligent tutoring system is more effective than an unintelligent tutoring program based on the same learning model (Nathan and Resnick, 1994).

Computers and construction

Just as in developmental and educational psychology more generally, advocates of associationist conceptions of learning with computers found themselves confronted with radically different conceptions of development and learning emanating from Piagetian theory. From a constructivist standpoint, of course, the key to education lies not in shaping behaviours, but in providing the conditions in which children themselves can construct an understanding of their world. The teacher is seen, not as instructor, but as facilitator, providing a stimulating and encouraging environment for intellectual exploration. In just the same way, within this tradition the role of the computer is not to teach but rather to afford opportunities for constructive activity.

Papert (1980, 1994) in particular has argued that the potential of the computer lies in extending children's control over their own learning. The computer should not be programming the child, he argued, rather the child should be programming the computer. To this end, Papert developed a modular programming language called Logo, suitable for use by even quite young children. Programming in Logo is seen as linking the child's intuitive grasp of how to do things in the world with the development of abstract levels of understanding of the same phenomena.

Working with the computer in this way is seen as having the potential to foster 'powerful ideas', in the form of generalisable thinking and problem-solving skills. We saw in Chapter 1 that Piaget held the view that children cannot develop their thinking as effectively in interactions with adults as they can with their peers because of the confounding effects of adult authority. The same stance is reflected in Papert's assertion that children's Logo programmes should not be judged right or wrong according to the canons of adult authority. Rather, the program either works or it doesn't. If it doesn't, a process of 'de-bugging' is required, which involves critically re-appraising the way it has been constructed.

Logo has established a place for itself in schools, but mainly as a useful approach to learning some aspects of mathematics (e.g. Hoyles and Sutherland, 1989). As far as fostering generalisable problem-solving skills is concerned, evidence of success is limited to situations in which Logo is used in the context of an intensive and highly structured curriculum, put together with this aim in mind (Pea and Kurland, 1984; De Corte, Verschaffel and Schrooten, 1992).

The constructivist approach to learning is evident in a number of other approaches to computer-based learning. An emphasis on 'learning by doing', and on using the computer as a vehicle for spontaneous exploratory learning is apparent in the recent enthusiasm for adventure games and simulations. Schank and Cleary (1995), for example, draw an analogy with flight simulators, which assist pilots to learn to fly by providing realistic environments without all the risks and costs of the real thing. In much the same way, they argue, other types of experience can be simulated on the computer, allowing children to play, experiment and explore, and greatly extending the range of things children can learn by doing.

Multimedia computer simulations can allow children to explore the inside of the human body, or the outer reaches of the universe. 'Alternative' worlds can be simulated, in which, for example, different laws of motion apply (Smith, 1991). Developments in the technology of virtual reality may extend the possibilities of such 'simulated worlds' very rapidly in the future. Equally, other developments in the field of hypermedia are already bringing to the classroom a much wider range of learning resources, along with an educational philosophy which stresses the need to 'put the learner in control' (Hutchins, Hall and Colbourn, 1993).

Computers and collaboration

As we saw in Chapter 1, in developmental psychology Piagetian constructivism has been somewhat overtaken by a social constructivist agenda identified with Vygotsky's ideas. Similarly, in the field of computers and learning the social dimensions of computer use are increasingly coming to centre stage.

Whereas early advocates of computer use in schools emphasised the benefits of individualising the learning process, in practice, things have turned out rather differently. In the 1980s classroom observational studies and surveys began to suggest that most educational use of computers in practice involves pairs or small groups, rather than individuals, and that these pairs or small groups often work relatively independently of the class teacher (e.g. Cummings, 1985; Jackson, Fletcher and Messer, 1986). Some classroom-based studies have claimed that small groups focused around a computer task are able to sustain task-related interaction better than similar groups working on non-computer tasks (e.g. Scanlon, Issroff and Murphy, 1999).

Experimental evaluations of collaborative as against individual modes of learning with computers stem from a number of different research traditions, and relate to a number of different types of computer-based learning experience. Already in the pre-computer 'teaching machine' literature, there was evidence that, despite the supposed importance of self-pacing, students learned as well or better in small groups as when working on their own (Hartley, 1968; Hartley and Hogarth, 1971).

Likewise in the context of CAI, despite the importance often attached to students working at their own individual level and pace, there is evidence that average individual learning outcomes are better for children who work together in pairs than for children who work alone (Mevarech, Silber and Fine, 1991).

If we turn to programming, we saw in our earlier discussion that the key claim made for Logo was that it supported the development by the individual of generalisable thinking skills, but that evidence in support of this claim is scant (Clements, 1987; Kliman, 1985). However, a number of studies with Logo and other programming languages have found evidence that peer interaction can facilitate children's achievements in programming. Children programming in Logo collaboratively have been found to do better than individuals on a variety of criteria (Healy, Pozzi and Hoyles, 1995; Clements and Nastasi, 1992), and the quality of social interaction and discussion has been shown to predict achievement in terms of eventual individual programming skills in Basic (Webb, Ender and Lewis, 1986).

A shift from a 'Piagetian' to a 'Vygotskian' perspective in considering computers and learning is further reflected in a recognition, supported by qualitative studies of computer use in authentic learning environments (Crook, 1994; Mercer, 1995, Schofield, 1995), that collaborative modes of learning involve teachers as well as peers, and that they take place in social and institutional frameworks. For the moment, though, our own focus will remain on the experimental analysis of peer interaction and learning in the context of children's computer use. We hope to show, through the studies described in the following chapters, how such studies can be used to expose and explore something of the complexity of the social bases of children's learning.

4 Kings, Crowns and Honeybears: a second series of studies

Introduction

In this chapter we shall describe a series of experimental studies based on the collaborative use of computer-based planning tasks. The studies are linked by the particular type of task used. Rather than start from existing tasks, as in the first series of studies (Chapter 2), we decided to develop our own. Instead of relying on computer simulations of non-computer tasks, such as the Tower of Hanoi or the balance beam, we wanted to develop a task which would better exploit the potential of the computer. We also wanted a task which would allow a more extended experience of solo or collaborative problem solving, rather than a sequence of quick trials.

We were interested by evidence from Rogoff and colleagues (Gauvain and Rogoff, 1989; Radziszewska and Rogoff, 1988) that the 'metacognitive' processes involved in successful planning (e.g. conscious, explicit monitoring and careful control of plan development) might lend themselves particularly well to facilitation through interaction, discussion and collaboration. We were also aware of evidence that 'adventure games' seemed to offer particularly stimulating contexts for peer discussion and interaction (Crook, 1987; Johnson and Johnson, 1986).

The task we designed lies somewhere along a continuum running from genuinely open adventure games to closed logical problems of the Tower of Hanoi type that we had used previously. We wanted a well-structured problem, but one which at the same time offered a variety of routes to solution, some more efficient than others. We were also seeking to capture several important aspects common to many situations of learning with computers. For example, computers may often hold a large amount of information which needs to be located and used systematically as a basis for completing the given task. The information is used as a basis for formulating a plan, which may then need to be amended in the light of feedback in the course of doing the task. We felt that this combination of information searching and planning was likely to figure prominently amongst the skills needed to work and learn with computers.

The first King and Crown study

The King and Crown task is a route-planning task implemented in Hypercard on a Macintosh computer. Whilst the underlying problem is fairly simple, the task as a whole is quite complex, as successful completion requires the user to search for relevant information, plan a solution and react constructively to any obstacles encountered along the way. The scenario is a quest involving the retrieval of a crown from an island. The users are told that: 'The King lives in his castle in Ashlan. He wants his crown and all his subjects (the driver, the guard, the pilot and the captain) in Ashlan for a feast. He wants you to give the orders to get them all there.'

The initial screen shows a map on which there are a number of 'buttons' marked by rectangles (see Figure 4.1). When the mouse-driven cursor is positioned over and then clicked on one of these buttons, further screens are presented. Thus if the user clicks on a place name, a screen appears which allows the user (via further buttons) to access information concerning the objects, persons and means of transport present at that particular location.

Users can also gather information by using the 'Info' button, which accesses a general information screen (see Figure 4.2). This offers an alternative way of obtaining information. If, for example, the users click on the button marked 'Pilot' on the 'Info' screen, they will obtain another screen allowing them to obtain information about what the pilot can do and/or to discover his whereabouts (see Figure 4.3). The highly embedded nature of these information resources means that users are given only the information they specifically ask for, and also that we can keep track of exactly what information they have obtained, and when.

The 'Goal' button makes available a written statement of the goal or aim of the game, whilst the 'Key' button makes available information on the various route markings. Thus, through an extended process of information searching, the users can discover the initial whereabouts of the characters, the crown and the different means of transport. In fact in the standard version of the task the driver, guard, pilot and captain all turn out to be initially at Ashlan. The crown is on the island of Fruggle, however, and so needs to be retrieved. There is a car at Ashlan, a ship at Brockley, another ship at Crowmarket and a plane on the island of Hushley.

When the users think they have sufficient information, they can initiate a move by clicking on the 'Act' button. This accesses the screen shown in

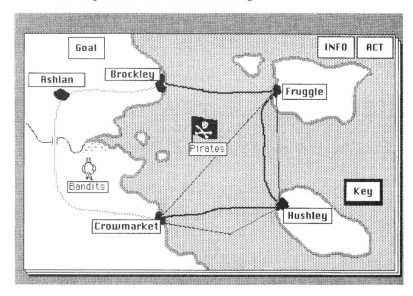

Figure 4.1 King and Crown software: the map

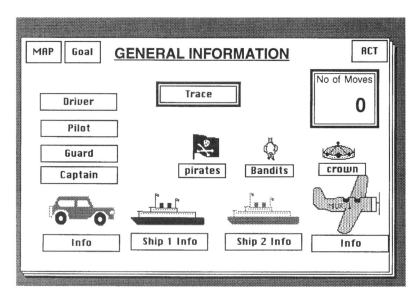

Figure 4.2 King and Crown software: the general information screen

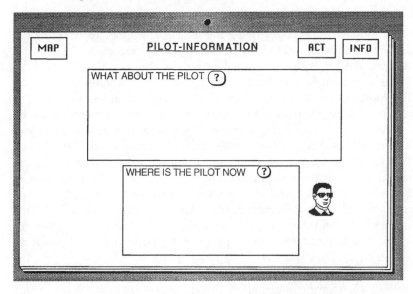

Figure 4.3 King and Crown software: the pilot information screen

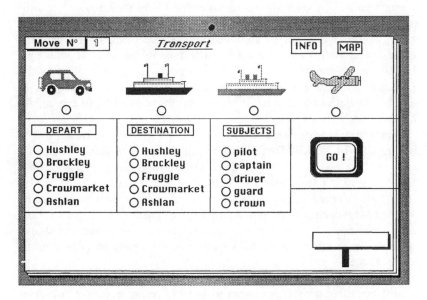

Figure 4.4 King and Crown software: the action screen

Figure 4.4. They are then required to specify the point of departure, a destination, the characters being moved (and whether or not they are moving the crown) and the means of transport being used. The move is then made by clicking on 'Go'.

The task is made complicated by the presence of bandits and pirates. The bandits will steal the crown on the mainland unless the guard is present. The pirates will steal the crown from any ship sailing the sea even if the guard is present. If the users obtained this information at the outset and thought it through, they could correctly conclude that the crown must be retrieved by plane. However, the plane can only carry a pilot and one passenger, which complicates things further. The optimal solution, in fact, is to take the car (and driver, guard, captain and pilot) to Crowmarket; to take the ship (and captain and pilot) to Hushley; to take the plane (and the pilot and the captain) to Fruggle to collect the crown; to return to Crowmarket, and then for all to return by car to Ashlan. This represents a total of five moves.

The software (initially developed by Richard Joiner) automatically updates all relevant information as each move is made. Thus at any point the children can stop and take stock of where the characters and means of transport are. Whilst in theory this might not be necessary, in practice it usually is. Most users, at least initially, either set off in the wrong direction or take the wrong characters, and thus encounter difficulties. If the users attempt to make a move which is impossible, or which would lead to the pirates stealing the crown, they get a warning message and are prevented from actually making the move. This means that the users then have to replan the move, to take account of the particular problem they have encountered. The task is thus a difficult one. Nevertheless most users, whether children or adults, find it engaging and highly motivating.

In an initial study using the 'King and Crown' software we set out to investigate whether children of around eleven years of age would profit from working collaboratively on this task (Blaye, Light, Joiner and Sheldon, 1991). First we wanted to know whether, on a task such as this which makes heavy demands on information management and planning skills, those working in pairs would perform better than those working alone. Second, we wanted to see to what extent any advantage shown by the pairs would transfer to a subsequent assessment of individual performance.

The study involved thirty-nine eleven-year-old children. They were taken from their school classroom to another room in the school either in pairs or individually (thirteen pairs and thirteen individuals). The decision as to which should work alone and which in pairs was made randomly. Allocation to particular pairs was also random except that pairs were always same-gender, and the teacher's advice was taken so as to avoid pairing children who actively disliked one another.

The children sat at the computer, which was controlled by mouse only. A video camera stood nearby on a tripod, and all paired sessions were videotaped. Children were given a scripted introduction to the object of the task, and (if necessary) to using a mouse. They were given a brief demonstration of how to obtain information and how to make a move, and completed a short practice task. They were provided with a paper copy of the map for reference, and encouraged to share the mouse and to work together to solve the problem.

The children were given thirty minutes to work on the task, during which time the researcher was present but very much in the background. They were told in advance not to worry if they didn't finish it, as they would have another go the next week. A week later they did have a second session, in pairs or individually just as in the first session. The task was the same, starting at the beginning again, and this time they had twenty-five minutes (unless they succeeded before this). They were told to try to complete the task in as few moves as possible.

A week later again, all children had a third session, but this time all of them worked individually. The task was also slightly different, in that the characters and means of transport were not all in the same places at the outset. The children were told about this before they started. This was done to ensure that the children could not succeed just by following a formula remembered from a previous session. They were given twenty minutes maximum on this post-test session.

On the first session, none of the thirteen children who worked alone succeeded in achieving the goal within the time limit. Two of the thirteen pairs (15 per cent) succeeded. On the second session, 15 per cent of the individuals and 46 per cent of the pairs succeeded, a difference which reached statistical significance. On the third session all children worked alone. Of those who had previously worked in pairs, 72 per cent succeeded, whereas of those who had worked alone throughout, only 31 per cent succeeded. Again, this difference was statistically reliable.

Examination of the computer logs made it clear that most children made initial moves without any clear idea where they were leading. They usually had to retrace them when it became apparent that they had not got the right personnel or means of transport available. By the second session there was evidence of more planning, significantly more so in the case of the children working in pairs. In fact all thirteen pairs got as far as moving the crown on the second session, but only three of the thirteen individuals did so.

Close scrutiny of the strategies adopted suggests that very few of the children even in this second session actually planned out a successful strategy in advance. In fact ten of the pairs and eleven of the individuals tried to move the crown by ship, but were stopped in their tracks by the warning message about the pirates. The difference between pairs and individuals was that, following this setback, six of the pairs but only two of the individuals immediately turned their attention to the plane. Thus it seems that the advantage of the pairs may lie more in adaptive *re*-planning than in thorough *pre*-planning.

The videotapes were analysed in terms of who, within the pairs, controlled the mouse most, and how decisions were made. Mouse control in the paired sessions (sessions one and two) turned out not to be correlated with score on the individual post-test (session three), so it did not seem that this aspect of the interaction was strongly related to ability or learning. However, the lack of an individual pre-test meant we were unable to rule out the possibility that improvement was related to the extent of mouse control.

Decisions regarding the destination for the next move, or who was to be taken, or what means of transport was to be used, were examined for all pairs in the second session. Intercoder reliability was checked on a random sample of six pairs. A particular child was identified as the author of a particular decision if he or she acted without reference to the partner or suggested a choice which the partner acted on. Intercoder reliability was a little over 80 per cent. Each of the children involved was thus given a 'decision score' based on the proportion of all decisions that child was responsible for. Decision score did turn out to be significantly correlated (−0.45) with individual performance on the third session. The children who controlled more of the decisions in the second session tended to do better as individuals on the third. Decision score was not related to any tendency to control the mouse more when working with a partner.

Decisions which were formulated simultaneously, or where both partners contributed some part of the formulation, were coded as shared decisions. It is interesting that shared decisions were significantly more prevalent in pairs in which both partners subsequently succeeded on their own. Pairs can also be scored in terms of the extent of disparity in the decision scores of their members. If we look back to the crucial point in the task alluded to earlier, where pairs were confronted with the impossibility of taking the crown by ship, it turns out that the six pairs who 'adaptively replanned' to take the plane at that point were the six with the lowest decision disparities. This suggests that it is not just having a partner that makes the difference, but having a fairly symmetrical relationship with that partner as far as decision making is concerned.

The videotapes also allowed us to see something of the patterning of role differentiation across time on the task. The mouse could only be held by one child at a time, but the paper map tended to be kept by the child who was not holding the mouse at that time. By channelling certain kinds of executive control into one role, the mouse may be seen as opening up a complementary role of 'navigator' or 'strategist'. A ready analogy might be two people driving around a strange town looking for an address; one could be attending to the minutiae of driving the car, while the other works at how to reach the destination.

Some researchers have commented on the potential disadvantages of role differentiations of this kind, which may lead to a child mastering only part of what is required to complete a task (e.g. Sheingold, Hawkins and Char, 1984; Hoyles and Sutherland, 1989). This did not appear to be a problem here, perhaps because having been encouraged to share the mouse, the children exchanged roles fairly frequently. Both Sheingold *et al.* and Hoyles and Sutherland were describing much longer sequences of interaction in classroom settings. It may be that over longer periods and with less supervision, the children tend to settle into less-than-productive patterns of role division. Interface and task characteristics may also be important in shaping such patterns.

It should also be acknowledged that other, less cognitive factors may also be involved. The success of ex-pair members on the third session could reflect increased self-confidence based on the prior experience of paired success. More generally, the presence of a partner on the first two sessions may have significant affective and/or motivational effects which may in turn have consequences for performance. We shall return to these issues later.

To summarise the results of this study, then, we can say that (i) the children working in pairs were at least twice as likely to succeed on the King and Crown task as the individuals, and (ii) the children who had previously worked in pairs on the task were at least twice as likely to succeed on the post-task variant of the King and Crown task as those who had worked alone throughout. Since the task was novel for all children at the beginning, success cannot rest on what they knew at the outset. We are looking at how an understanding of the task domain, the ways of acting within that domain, and the solution strategy have been built up more or less successfully over some seventy-five minutes of computer-based work. On the basis of this study it seems that peer interaction can play a significant part in the construction of this kind of understanding, even without the kind of 'forced interaction' (dual key controls, for example, see Chapter 2) which we had to resort to in the first series of studies.

The second King and Crown study

A second study was conducted to allow us to obtain a substantially larger sample of paired interactions for analysis. Our aim was to identify important aspects of the interaction, paying particular attention to the knowledge created and shared in the verbal interaction between the partners. We wanted to see whether we could relate measures of such verbal interaction to the outcomes for the pairs, and to the pair members' subsequent performance when working on their own.

Since our interest was in the kinds of interactions that were associated with more and less successful pairs, we did not use an individual comparison group in this study (Barbieri and Light, 1992). Also there were only two sessions. All of the children (eleven-year-olds again) worked in pairs in the first session. There were thirty-three pairs in all, eleven pairs of boys, eleven pairs of girls, and eleven mixed gender pairs. In the first session the children worked in pairs for twenty-five minutes. This session was video-recorded. In the second session all children worked individually with a variant of the task, as in the previous study.

The King and Crown software used was amended in several ways for this study. The bandits were eliminated, as was the guard. The automatic logging was refined to provide various summary measures, including a new measure of levels of success. These levels correspond to significant points of progression through the task, all being necessary to eventual success. Thus performance was categorised according to whether the children got no further than moving the car (level one), moving the ship (level two), moving the plane (level three), moving the crown (level four), getting the crown to the mainland (level five), or successfully completing the task (level six). The videotape transcripts, combined with the computer logs, allowed a fairly full picture to be built up of the children's interactions with one another and with the computer. The computer provides both information and feedback, and the ways in which these are integrated into the children's interactions was one of our chief concerns.

The categories developed for analysis are given in detail in Barbieri and Light (1992). Planning was operationalised as verbal reference to a sequence of moves or possible moves. For example: 'We've got to go to Ashlan to pick up the captain, and then we'll take the ship to Fruggle'. Negotiation was coded when a proposal from one child was opposed by the partner, and one or both parties went on to defend their point of view or attempt to overcome the contradiction. For example: 'Now, back to Brockley and Ashlan'; 'No, you can't'; 'Yes we can'; 'No, 'cos the pirates will get us'. Integration of information search was coded when children drew explicit conclusions from the information they obtained from the computer, integrating it into a plan of action. Similarly, integration of error messages was coded when explicit statements of implication were drawn on the basis of error (or warning) messages received from the computer. All these codes were assigned to pairs (i.e. to segments of conversation between the two children), rather than to individuals.

The results revealed that planning was the most successful of the interaction measures in terms of its relationship with levels of performance, correlating +0.6 with the level of success of the pair on session one, and +0.4 with the level of individual success (averaged across the two partners) on session two. Integration of information search showed lower, but still significant, correlations, at +0.4 and +0.3 respectively. Negotiation correlated with paired (+0.3) but not individual performance, while integration of error messages correlated only with individual performance (+0.3).

Another way to look at the data is in terms of the relationships between the interaction measures and the 'pairwise patterns' of success in session two. The ex-members of any given pair might both succeed (SS), they might both fail (FF), or one may fail whilst the other succeeds (FS). For this purpose, performance levels one to three were treated as failure whilst levels four to six were considered as success.

When we look at the prevalence of the different forms of verbal interaction across these three pair-outcome types, an interesting pattern emerges. The SS pairs show significantly higher levels of planning, negotiation and integration of information search than either the FS or the FF pairs. There is no difference on any of the interaction measures between the FS and FF pairs. By contrast, if we look at the levels of success achieved by the pairs at session one, it is the FS and SS pairs which look similar, scoring significantly better than the FF pairs. It seems, then, that the FS pairs are characterised in session one by a low level of constructive verbal interaction relative to their level of achievement. The achievement, one assumes, rests upon the performance of the more capable child, but they are not succeeding in building a shared understanding of the task.

It seems, then, that the verbal measures designed to index planning, negotiation and the coconstruction of knowledge do relate significantly to successful problem solving by the pairs, and to learning outcomes as indexed by the subsequent success of individual children in the second session. However, to be fully confident that these associations reflect causal processes we would really need access to appropriate pre-test measures of a kind which were not available in this study. We shall return to other findings from this study when discussing gender issues in the next chapter. Here we shall move on to a third and final piece of research conducted with the King and Crown task, this time with adults.

The third King and Crown study

This small scale study was conducted by Agnes Blaye with students at a French university, using a French language version of the software (Blaye and Light, 1995). The students had two sessions with the task, working either in pairs throughout (five pairs) or individually throughout (six individuals). On the first session only two of the individuals got as far as moving the ship, and none moved the plane, whereas all the pairs moved the ship and one pair got as far as moving the plane. On the second session only one individual succeeded in retrieving the crown, whereas all of the pairs did.

Although small, this study is of interest for two reasons. First, it is notable that the task itself seems to work just as well for undergraduates as for eleven year olds, and indeed causes them nearly as much difficulty. Of course there may be cohort effects; when the eleven-year-olds we tested in the first two studies reach university they may have gone beyond this kind of thing! Secondly, it is interesting to see that the peer advantage which marked the results of the first King and Crown study is apparent here too, with university students, although we have no individual post-test measure in this case.

Even at session two, more than one third of the moves attempted by the students working alone failed, either because they had not specified all the parameters or because they were attempting something that was impossible. No such difficulties occurred amongst the pairs. The students working alone also made a considerable number of redundant information searches, that is, searches for information that they had already in fact obtained. This accounted for 31 per cent of the information searched by the individuals on the first session and 25 per cent of that searched by individuals on the second session. The corresponding figures for redundant information searches by pairs were significantly lower, at 8 per cent and 0 per cent. This points to the conclusion that the pairs were better at remembering what they had done and what they had found out; another important aspect of building a shared representation of the task.

The various analyses conducted across the three King and Crown studies have offered some leads concerning the factors influencing successful learning, but the significance of many of these cannot really be assessed without having some idea of the initial competencies of the individuals, prior to the experience of working together. To address these issues we conducted a much larger study, building in pre- as well as post-tests. At the same time, we made changes in procedures. Most importantly, we changed the nature of the 'individual' conditions, as will be described below. We also developed a new version of the software, which we called 'Honeybears'.

The first Honeybears study

The Honeybears task was designed to eliminate some of the more obviously male-stereotyped elements of the King and Crown task, for reasons discussed in more detail in the next chapter. The underlying structure of the Honeybears task is, however, exactly the same as the King and Crown task. In the Honeybears version, the scenario is that three bears (referred to as the 'honeybears') have set out for a picnic at Almwood, and discover that they have forgotten their honey. The honey is on an island at the other side of the river, but in the river there are honeymonsters who will steal the honey if the bears attempt to retrieve it by boat (honeymonsters figured at the time on advertisements for a popular honey-coated breakfast cereal, so the children could conjure up an image of them quite easily). The presence of the honeymonsters necessitated the retrieval of the honey by air. In this scenario we used a pony rather than a car, a rowing boat rather than a ship, and a hot air balloon rather than a plane. Each of the bears was able to handle one of these means of transport, so we had 'ponybear', 'waterbear' and 'airbear'.

The basic map screen is shown in Figure 4.5. The optimal solution involves (i) taking all three bears by pony from Almwood to Cob, (ii) taking 'airbear' and 'waterbear' to Hilt by boat, (iii) taking both on to Flint by balloon, (iv) returning by balloon to Cob with the honey, and (v) bringing all three bears and the honey back to Almwood by pony. Thus, whilst the Honeybears and the King and Crown tasks differ with respect to the context in which the problem is set (and also with respect to certain minor interface characteristics), both present the same problem in the same adventure game format and call for an identical solution strategy.

For the first study using the 'Honeybears' variant of the software (Littleton, Light, Joiner, Messer and Barnes, 1992), we incorporated an individual pre-test session to provide us with an index of each child's initial level of competence. This makes it possible to take account of antecedent differences in children's competence when examining the association between task performance and other variables. The incorporation of such a session also allows us to assess the extent to which differences in outcome might reflect antecedent differences in the relative abilities of the two members making up a given pair. The study also incorporated an 'individual' condition, allowing us to compare the performance of those who had worked in pairs at some stage with those who worked alone throughout.

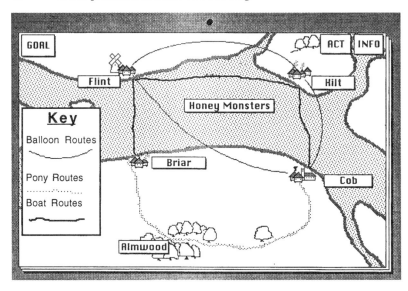

Figure 4.5 Honeybears software: the map

From observation in the context of other studies, we had reason to suppose that some of the children who worked at the computer alone in the first session were apprehensive, and we wanted to make the situation more 'user friendly'. Since we by now had the resources to set up four computers in the schools instead of one, we took children from the classroom in fours. Where they were to work alone, each sat at a computer and worked without conferring with the others. Where they were to work in pairs, members of each pair sat together at a computer, and the other two machines went unused. The positioning of the computers around the periphery of the classroom was such that the screen of each was visible only to its user(s). Nevertheless, the children were always working in the presence of other children who were similarly engaged.

One hundred and twenty eleven and twelve-year-olds took part in the study. The first stage involved each of them having a fifteen minute session working on their own with Honeybears. From this we were able to derive an index of each child's initial level of ability on the task. The second stage, which took place a week later, consisted of a thirty-minute session in which the children once again worked on the Honeybears task. Thirty of the children continued to work alone and the others worked with a partner.

Children's performance at the first stage was not used in assigning children to conditions for the second. Children were allocated at random to the paired or individual conditions, and then within the group of children allocated to paired conditions, their teachers were invited to suggest pairings of children who could be expected to work well together. Children working as a pair always came from the same school class. There were forty-five pairs in all, with a mix of within-gender and between-gender pairings (this aspect of the study will be picked up in Chapter 5). At the third stage of the study, a week later, all 120 children were post-tested individually in a twenty-minute session using a variant of the Honeybears task in which initial locations were changed.

The children's performance on the task was measured using a revised version of the scoring system employed in the second King and Crown study. This new scoring system introduced a level 0, which indicates that the children had failed to make a move at all. Levels one to six remained unchanged, whilst levels seven and eight were added to give extra credit to children who completed the task either more quickly or in a smaller number of moves.

Figure 4.6 shows the overall results, comparing those who worked alone throughout with those who were paired for the second stage. Predictably, given the random allocation to conditions, there was no difference in performance between the groups at the first stage. Figure 4.6 suggests that there was an advantage for pairs over individuals at the second stage, but that there was no carry-over of this advantage to individual post-test performance.

Since we now have individual pre-test performance measures, we can test the significance of the pair advantage by looking at the relative improvement of those who worked in pairs as against those who worked alone. An analysis based on change of score from first to second stage showed a significant advantage for those who worked in pairs. An alternative statistical procedure using the mean change score for each pair yielded a similar result.

Mean performance at the post-test stage was somewhat poorer than at the second stage. However, it needs to be remembered that the post-test used a variant of the task, and also allowed less time. The important observation is that, in contrast with the findings of the first King and Crown study, we have no evidence here of a benefit at post-test for those children who had earlier worked in pairs.

As noted earlier, the allocations of children to particular pairs at stage two were made without regard to the children's pre-test (stage one) scores. Consequently, some children were assigned to a partner who had scored the same as they had themselves at pre-test. These may be termed 'symmetrical' pairs. Other children were assigned to pairs in which there was a difference of one performance level in the pre-test ('asymmetrical'

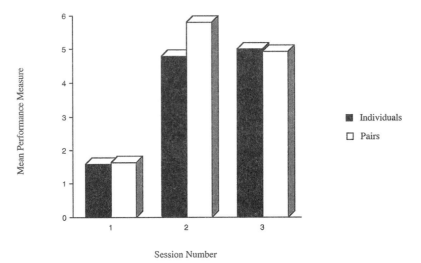

Session Number

Figure 4.6 The mean level of performance for the 'pairs' and 'individuals' during each of the three sessions

pairs). In others there was a difference of more than one level in the pre-test performance of the pair members ('highly asymmetrical' pairs).

As it turned out, the pairs established at stage two actually comprised fourteen symmetrical pairs, twenty-three asymmetrical pairs and eight highly asymmetrical pairs. We analysed the progress made (from stage one to stage three) for members of each of these types of pair. The average improvement in performance level from stage one to stage three averaged 3.8 for members of symmetrical pairs, 2.9 for members of asymmetrical pairs and 2.4 for members of highly asymmetrical pairs. This difference proved to be statistically significant overall. The outcome for the symmetrical pairs was significantly better than for either of the other two groups.

As a check on this rather striking result, we went on to examine the performance of a sub-sample of children who all started from the same pre-test level. The modal pre-test score (level one) was used for this purpose. Thus, one group consisted of those children whose pre-test score was one and who were paired with a child whose pre-test score was less than their own (n = 7). Another group consisted of those whose pre-test score was one and whose partners' score was greater than their own (n = 16). The third group were those whose partner also scored one at pre-test (n = 12).

Figure 4.7 shows the results of a comparison between these three groups. The best stage two performance came from those children work-

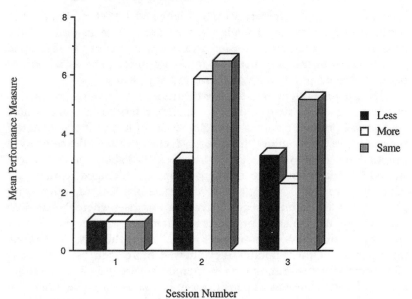

Session Number

Figure 4.7 The mean session 1, 2 and 3 performance of the 'same', 'less' and 'more' able pairings

ing as symmetrical pairs. By stage three the performance levels were lowest for those who had been paired with a more able partner, not significantly better for those who had been paired with a less able partner, but significantly better for those with a partner of the same initial ability.

This analysis indicates that 'symmetrical pairings' (where the children are of the same initial level of ability) function better than 'asymmetrical pairings' (where the children are of different initial levels of ability), both in terms of pair performance and in terms of individual learning outcomes. With a task like this where the participants are all 'starting from scratch' and having to grapple with complex information (and an unfamiliar interface), it seems that a balance of initial abilities may hold the best promise of a good learning outcome.

Some light is thrown on the processes underpinning this 'symmetry advantage' by an analysis undertaken using an approach to interaction analysis based on that of Roschelle and Teasley (1995). These authors approached collaboration in terms of the construction of a 'joint problem space', and offered an analysis based on a single pair of how knowledge is introduced into the emerging joint problem space, and how divergences in meaning are monitored and 'repaired'. We applied a similar approach to four of the pairs from the present study, two 'symmetrical' and two 'asymmetrical' pairs (Joiner, Messer, Light and Littleton, 1994). The symmetrical pairs selected made good progress, both in terms of the performance of the pair in session two and in terms of the individual performances of the pair members in session three. The asymmetrical pairs performed poorly both as a pair and at post-test.

Four categories were used to code the transcripts of verbal interaction in these pairs. The first of these, 'Repairs', refers to instances where conflicts of view are resolved through the use of justifications, counter-suggestions or elaborations (this category is close to our earlier category of negotiation). A second category concerned 'Collaborative sentences', started by one partner and finished by another. Related to these are 'Collaborative plans', where one child starts a plan and the other completes it. Finally, 'Simultaneous utterances' are cases where the children make essentially the same utterance simultaneously. The symmetrical/successful pairs showed somewhat more of all of these types of verbal interaction, but most notably they showed more than twice as many Collaborative plans. Simultaneous utterances were present in the transcripts of both symmetrical pairs (four in one and five in the other) but were absent altogether in the asymmetrical pairs.

These results have to be treated with caution, given the limited sample involved, but they closely echo those reported earlier (first King and Crown study) relating to shared decision making in successful pairs. Our finding of superior performance and learning in symmetrical as compared with asymmetrical pairings is consistent with the findings of some other researchers (e.g. Whitelock, O'Shea, Taylor, Scanlan, Clark and O'Malley, 1993), but inconsistent with others (e.g. Howe, Tolmie, Anderson and Mackenzie, 1992). It seems likely that the key factor is how far success on the task depends upon prior knowledge that the participants bring to the interaction.

However, the most striking result of this first Honeybears study was the negative one, namely that, overall, the children who worked in pairs on the task at stage two were *not* significantly better at post-test than those children who worked alone throughout. Given that this result runs directly contrary to what had been established in the first King and Crown study, we were obviously concerned to establish what made the difference.

Though the software in use was different, the task was formally isomorphic with the previous one, and the task remained a difficult one. The lack of differentiation of outcomes was certainly not accounted for by a ceiling effect. The pairs did do significantly better at stage two, when actually working together, though this effect is a modest one which reaches statistical significance only because of the large numbers of participants in this study. One hypothesis might be that the lack of stage three (post-test) advantage for those who worked in pairs might have arisen because, by contrast with the first King and Crown study, the children in the present study all worked alone at the first (pre-test) stage. Thus the degree of differentiation between the paired and individual conditions was less in this study. It is also possible that the fact that children meet the task first on their own, and only later in pairs, alters the dynamics of the children's interaction with the task.

However, there is another design difference which offers a possible explanation for the difference in outcome, and one which lends itself more readily to testing. This concerns the way in which the 'individual' sessions were handled. As noted earlier, whereas the children working individually in the King and Crown studies were alone with an adult experimenter and a computer, those in this study were always in a room with three others classmates working on the same task. There was no opportunity for overt interaction between the children during the session, but might this simple fact of peer presence have made a difference? There is some suggestive evidence on this point from a study of secondary school physics students using a computer simulation (Whitelock, et al., 1993). These authors report a facilitation effect when students worked in the presence of others, even without interaction, as compared with working entirely on their own. The next study was designed as a direct check on whether this kind of facilitation was occurring here.

The second Honeybears study

A further study using the Honeybears software was set up to investigate the possibility that peer presence, even without interaction, might be a factor underlying the facilitatory effect of pairing (Light, Littleton, Messer and Joiner, 1994). Thirty-two eleven year olds, sixteen boys and sixteen girls, participated in the study. Half of the boys and half of the girls were allocated to a 'peer absence' condition. These children were withdrawn from the classroom individually, and were given a single thirty-minute session working with the Honeybears task on their own, with only the adult experimenter present. The other half (allocation being random) were assigned to a 'peer presence' condition. These children were withdrawn from the classroom in same-sex groups of four, and given a single session on the Honeybears task working in the same room as one another but without interaction. This second condition resembled that for the first Honeybears study, the machines being arranged so that the children could not see one another's screens. Care was taken to keep the form of introduction and all the instructions constant across the two conditions.

The results of this study were striking. The mean performance level for the children who worked in the presence of others (2.9) was significantly better than the performance of those who worked alone (1.8). Thus quite apart from any consequences of productive verbal or practical interaction between partners working together on the task, we have here evidence for the operation of a quite different kind of social facilitation of performance, which depends simply on the presence of classmates working on the same task.

Overview

The three studies using the King and Crown software gave a more encouraging picture of the benefits of peer interaction than the studies using standard problem-solving tasks reviewed in Chapter 2. With this more open and extended type of problem solving (arguably more 'face valid' in relation to educational experiences), the present studies seem to show that both children and adults can reap considerable benefit from the presence of a collaborating partner. This peer advantage was evident even though the children were given no more than a general invitation to work collaboratively, without being forced into any particular pattern of interaction through the instructions or the structuring of the task itself.

The first King and Crown study showed that the peer advantage could carry over to individual subsequent performance on a slight variant of the task. The second showed that the verbal interactions within the pair were predictive of pair performance, of the subsequent performance of the individual members of the pair, and indeed of the relative performance of members of the pair at post-test. The third attested to the age independence of at least some of the effects observed, and suggested that the more effective use of available information to build a shared representation of the task might be one factor explaining the advantage enjoyed by pairs.

The first Honeybears study was to have been the definitive one. Its scale, and full pre-test/post-test design, should have allowed a detailed analysis of the basis of paired advantage. The observation that symmetrical pairings were more effective than other pairings seems to support an interpretation couched broadly in terms of coconstruction rather than conflict. However, other studies (e.g. Howe and Tolmie, 1999, using tasks which focus on the judgements and prior knowledge that children bring to physics tasks) have found evidence that asymmetrical pairs are more effective. We should acknowledge that different psychological and interactive processes are likely to be brought into play by different types of task, and we should not seek to draw overgeneralised conclusions. The more important observation is that, as a whole, pairs did produce better performance than individuals, but did *not* produce better learning, as indexed by what the children could do by themselves at post-test.

The second Honeybears study lends support to an interpretation of this result which focuses not on the paired but on the 'individual' condition. It appears that the social setting of individual testing can have a marked effect on performance. The results echo those of Whitelock *et al.* (1993), and on the basis of informal observation we concur with their observation that it is not so much a case of facilitation of performance through the presence of peers working on the same task, as a matter of degradation of performance through anxiety when children work alone. Sitting as they were at a novel computer, faced with a novel task under the watchful gaze of an unfamiliar adult, it is perhaps not surprising that some of the individuals appeared anxious and had difficulty engaging with the task. From an experimental psychologist's point of view, this type of individual condition represents a natural and appropriate control condition against which to assess the impact of social processes in the pairs. However, this neglects the social and emotional dimensions of the control condition itself which, as evidenced here, have a considerable bearing upon performance.

Though peer presence effects and related phenomena are by no means novel to social psychologists, their importance has been little recognised by developmental and educational psychologists. Whilst, as we saw in Chapter 1, there are differences between the Piagetian and Vygotskian approaches, one of their similarities is that they are both essentially cognitive in orientation. Neither has much to say about children's affective experience of the learning situation, or their motivation and self-confidence. To embrace the effects demonstrated in this final study, the sense in which we normally understand terms such as interaction or communication may need to be widened.

The next chapter will revisit the studies described in this chapter, adding others using the same software, with a focus on gender as a factor influencing children's responses. Some of the wider issues raised by the present studies, in terms of the more covert social processes that may be operating, are taken up in Chapter 6.

5   Gender agendas

Boys, girls and computers

Much of the research on peer interaction processes in learning originating in Piagetian and Vygotskian theories tends to be rather insensitive to the 'non-cognitive' characteristics of the individuals doing the learning. One characteristic of learners that has drawn some attention, however, is gender. This is especially true where the learning involves computers. Psychologists and educationalists alike are well aware of the danger that educational computer use might not just reflect, but actually amplify, pre-existing sex differences (Light, 1997; Littleton, 1995, Littleton and Bannert, in press).

Certainly girls often seem to be a good deal less enthusiastic about computer use than boys. Surveys suggest that more girls than boys have negative attitudes towards computers right across the school age range (Martin, 1991; Robertson, Calder, Fung, Jones and O'Shea, 1995; Todman and Dick, 1993, Whitley, 1997). A substantial proportion of both boys and girls seem to regard use of the computer as being more 'appropriate' for boys than for girls, and believe that boys like and use computers more than girls do (Hoyles, 1988; Hughes, Brackenridge and MacLeod, 1987; Wilder, Mackie and Cooper, 1985). Girls may hold to the view that 'girls in general' are just as computer competent as boys, while at the same time rating their own abilities lower than boys do (Shashaani, 1993).

An Australian study suggested that such sex differences in attitude were particularly influenced by a sub-group of girls who were intensely antagonistic to computers, while in general boys see computers as likely to play a larger part in their future careers than girls do (Hattie and Fitzgerald, 1988). International comparisons show that such sex differences in response to computers amongst students are widespread (Pelgrum and Plomp, 1993; Janssen Reinen and Plomp, 1997). If anything, this imbalance in response to computers has become stronger over the last decade or so (Newton and Beck, 1993), and differences seem to become more pronounced the longer the children are in school.

The picture in respect of 'voluntary' usage of computers is perhaps less clearcut, but not more cheering. Observational research suggests gender differences in usage are already evident in primary schools (Straker, 1989) and that levels of participation in computer-related activities amongst girls in UK secondary education tend to be low (Culley, 1988, 1993). This applied particularly strongly to optional computing activities such as computer clubs, where in some studies 90 per cent of participants have been found to be male. The proportion of girls entering for examinations in computer studies and computer science is low and, if anything, has tended to decline over time (Buckley and Smith, 1991; Culley, 1993; Hughes, 1990). Certainly recruitment of girls to UK university courses in computer science fell markedly during the 1980s (Hoyles, 1988). There is also recent evidence that the proportion of female relative to male Ph.D. students and lecturers in computer science departments is getting progressively smaller (Camp, 1997).

There is evidence from other settings too that boys are more likely to use computers than girls. Thus, for example, Greenfield (1995) has shown that in a science museum girls were more likely to use some of the interactive displays (especially puzzles), but boys were more likely to use those presented on computers. More importantly, home computers are more likely to be bought for boys than for girls, and where they are available, boys tend to use them more than girls for all purposes (Martin, 1991; Linnakylä, 1996). In one study it was found that ten times as many boys as girls had sole access to a computer at home (Robertson *et al.*, 1995). It is possible that greater familiarity with computers out of school contributes to the differences we see in school (Beynon, 1993). However, Giacquinta, Bauer and Levin (1993) found only a modest amount of general educational use of home computers (e.g. wordprocessing) and almost no use of the home computer to support study of school subjects. The authors point to a lack of liaison between home and school, and a lack of willingness on the part of parents to get involved with the computer, as being the main contributory factors. Home computers were used mainly for game playing.

The 'macho' culture of computer games has often been commented upon (Provenzo, 1991), but some of the same features in fact characterise a good deal of educational software. Cooper, Hall and Huff (1990) observed that the most popular software in use for teaching maths and spelling employed the imagery of guns, missiles and warships, and adopted a competitive, aggressive format. It is obviously possible that gender stereotyping in the preferred formats of educational software might play a part in shaping gendered responses to computers.

Sex differences in children's preferred 'style' of working with computers have been noted in various studies. Thus, for example, it has been argued that while boys tend to adopt a more analytic and closed approach in working with computers, girls tend to adopt a more open-ended and exploratory approach (Turkle and Papert, 1990). Kirkup (1992) has suggested that, whilst either style is compatible with using computers for learning, software development for learning as well as for leisure has tended to follow a masculine path.

Another stylistic difference sometimes reported points to a natural linkage between the issue of sex differences in response to computers and the issue of peer interaction in learning. Girls, it has been suggested, prefer collaborative modes of working, while boys prefer to work alone (Dalton, 1990; Hoyles, 1988). Hoyles, Sutherland and Healy (1991) suggest that while boys seem to see interactions around the keyboard as time-consuming diversions, girls see them as affording opportunities for mutual support and the development of ideas. Observations in mixed sex classrooms suggest that, given the opportunity, boys tend to work individually at the computer, while girls tend to work cooperatively (Underwood and Underwood, 1999). When children do work in groups around the computer, girls tend to work more collaboratively than boys. The boys tend to get fractious, one result of which is that they get more of the teacher's attention than the girls do (Culley, 1993).

Mixing the sexes does not seem to help. A substantial literature points to the danger that boys will dominate mixed-sex interactions (Graddol and Swann, 1989; Swann, 1997). The research literature more specifically on mixed-sex groups (mainly pairs) working with computers suggests that these may indeed be relatively unproductive, with boys being socially dominant in such situations (Siann, Durndell, McLeod and Glissov, 1988). Watson refers to classroom observations such as: 'Boys came in first and sat squarely in front of the screen. I had to remind them to let girls have room to sit down' (1997, p. 221).

Underwood, McCaffery and Underwood (1990) found that while single-sex pairs did better than individuals when working on a sentence completion task, the same was not true for mixed-sex pairs. Underwood, Jindal and Underwood (1994) found that mixed-sex pairs of upper primary age children performed poorly on a computer-based language task, showing little evidence of cooperative working, even given encouragement to cooperate. Howe and Tolmie (1999) found with twelve to fifteen year olds working on a computer-based physics task that the amount of task-related talk (expressed as number of dialogue turns) was substantially lower in mixed-sex as compared to single-sex pairs. They also observed that such interaction as there was in the mixed-sex pairs was not related to learning outcomes in the way that interaction in single-sex pairs was.

With larger groups of nine- to twelve-year-olds (consisting of three boys and three girls) Pozzi, Healy and Hoyles (1993) did not find significant evidence of dominance. However, where groups fragmented, they did so along gender lines, and antagonism was always across gender lines. There are indications that larger mixed-sex groups may run very differently depending on the balance of males and females in the group, with equality or inequality of numbers being an important factor (Lee, 1993).

Evidence that girls actually learn less in the context of mixed-sex pairs is not particularly consistent. Pheasy and Underwood (1994) found only slightly lower levels of performance in mixed-sex as compared with same-sex pairs. Hughes and colleagues (Hughes, Brackenridge, Bibby and Greenhough, 1988; Hughes, Greenhough and Laing, 1992) found no difference in learning outcomes between single and mixed-sex pairings on a Logo task, except in one study where girls who had worked with boys actually outperformed those who had worked with other girls. It seems probable that the particular task involved has a good deal to do with the results observed.

As Swann (1997) observes, the 'boys dominate girls' position is an oversimplification. What happens depends on the task and the situation as well as on the participants. Fitzpatrick and Hardman (1994, and Fitzpatrick, 1996) sought to establish how far any distinctive features of mixed-sex task-focused interaction were specific to tasks involving computers. They devised two similar tasks involving language puzzles, one on a computer and one set within the context of a board game. Working with seven and nine year olds, they found that mixed-sex pairs were marked by significantly more 'assertive' interactions than single-sex pairs.

This applied both with the non-computer and the computer-based task. Interestingly, though, on the non-computer language task it was the girl who was more likely to initiate an assertive interaction, whereas with the computer task it was significantly more often the boy who acted assertively. Related to this was the observation that in the mixed-sex pairs the girls handled the dice and counters more often than the boys, but on the computer task the boys did the keying in more frequently than the girls.

The evidence from both observational and experimental studies thus suggests that boys exert a dominant influence in the context of mixed-sex encounters with computers. It has been reported that girls in single-sex schools have more positive attitudes to computers, and that in such schools computer studies courses are popular and computer clubs thrive (Culley, 1993; Gardner, McEwan and Curry, 1985). Taken together, these findings have led to enthusiasm in some quarters for segregating boys from girls in the context of computer use at school.

However, before leaving this review, it is important to note that there appears to be little evidence that boys actually perform better on computer-based tasks than girls, or that boys learn more than girls in the context of computer-based learning. There are plenty of experimental studies which report no significant difference in the achievements of boys and girls on computer-based tasks, including, for example, some of our own research on logic programming (Light and Colbourn, 1987). Likewise, although fewer girls take computer science courses and degrees, those that do take such courses perform well (Lockheed, Nielson and Stone, 1985). Thus the link between attitudes, choices, inter-actions and learning outcomes looks likely to be far from straightforward.

In this chapter, we shall first revisit the 'King and Crown' and 'Honeybears' studies described previously, attending to thus far unremarked sex differences in the children's performance. We shall then report some further studies which directly address sex differences in children's response to these two tasks. Finally we shall broaden the range of tasks under consideration and look at other aspects of gendered response to collaborative learning with computers.

Kings, Crowns, Honeybears and gender

The second of the King and Crown studies described in the previous chapter included a balance of boys and girls, with mixed-sex as well as same-sex pairs. There were eleven boy–boy pairs, eleven girl–girl pairs and eleven girl–boy pairs. The children worked as a pair in a first session and then individually (on a slight variant of the task) in a second session a week later. They were also given a brief attitude questionnaire after the second session. Seating positions and patterns of mouse control were coded from videotapes of the first (paired) session.

On the first session the levels of success were modest (median performance level 2) and there was no significant difference between the different types of pair. By the second session, when the children were working individually, however, a large sex difference became apparent (see Figures 5.1 and 5.2). Figure 5.1 shows that at session two the boys (median level six) were vastly better than the girls (median level two). Figure 5.2 shows the pattern according to pair type.

The children who had worked in boy–boy pairs did best, those who had worked in girl–girl pairs did worst, with the mixed pairs intermediate. But of course these last can be separated into boys and girls. When this is done, it emerges that the boys in the mixed-sex pairs had done as well as the boys in single-sex pairs, and the girls in mixed-sex pairs had done as

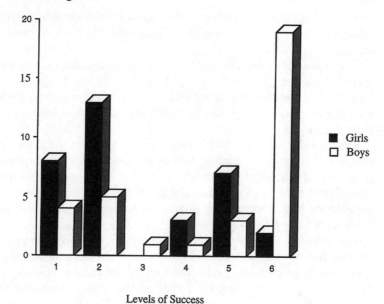

Figure 5.1 Success in session 2 by gender

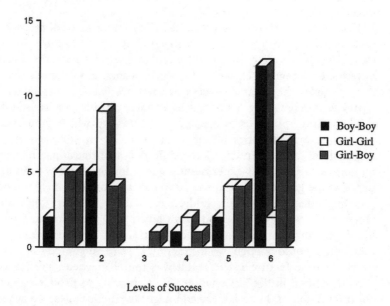

Figure 5.2 Success in session 2 by session 1 pair type

badly as those in the girl–girl pairs. We thus seem to see a substantial main effect for gender upon performance, but no effect of mixed versus single-sex pairing.

One of the post-experimental questionnaire items asked the children to indicate on a five-point scale how much they agreed or disagreed with the statement: 'I like working on my own more than with a partner'. Regardless of pair type, the boys tended to agree with the statement, the girls to disagree.

Seating positions were interesting. No attempt was made to regulate this, but it transpired that in the mixed-sex pairs the boys were significantly more likely than the girls to end up sitting in a position (on the left) which gave them right-handed access to the mouse. Whether this is because the boys sought out this chair or because the girls avoided it we are unable to say.

The children were given a general injunction to share the mouse, but the evenness of 'shares' was variable. The girl–girl pairs showed the most even distribution, the boy–boy pairs were intermediate, and the mixed-sex pairs showed the least even distribution. The median number of switches of mouse control between the members of girl–girl pairs in the course of the twenty-five minute session was eleven. In the boy–boy pairs the corresponding figure was four, and in the mixed pairs the median was zero. In most of these pairs the boy controlled the mouse throughout.

Thus there were quite marked sex differences in performance, and quite marked pair-type differences in some non-verbal aspects of behaviour. However, our attempts to differentiate the pairs using the categories of verbal exchange described in the previous chapter were not successful. For example, the greater success of the boys was not associated with significantly higher levels of verbally explicit planning or negotiation.

These findings led us to consider the extent to which the noticeably masculine characteristics of the King and Crown software might be responsible for the gender-related differences in the apparent learning outcomes. On the post-experimental questionnaire there was no indication that the girls were less attracted to the task, but this merely reflected a ceiling effect, in that all children tended to give very high ratings. Objectively, the task consisted of an adventure game in the form of a 'quest' in which male characters engaged in stereotypically male activities. What would happen, we wondered, if we re-versioned the task so as to avoid these features? The result was the Honeybears version of the task, described in the last chapter. In attempting to produce a gender-neutral version of the task we used images from fairy tales and advertisements. Some commentators (e.g. Fitzpatrick, 1996) see the resulting scenario as distinctively feminine in orientation, but it was not our intention to achieve this. Rather, we wanted something which was non-masculine.

The first Honeybears study, as described in the previous chapter, afforded an opportunity to look at both gender and pair-type effects once again with this new software. In the first (pre-test) session all children worked alone (or rather, they worked one-to-a-computer without interaction, in groups of four). In the second session, the children were assigned at random to boy–boy, girl–boy or girl–girl pairs, there being fifteen of each pair type. On a final (post-test) session they worked on their own again, as in the pre-test.

Figure 5.3 shows the pattern of performance of the three pair types across the three sessions. The overall performance of the boy–boy pairs was slightly better than that of the girl–girl pairs, with the mixed pairs intermediate, but the differences both at session two (when the children were working in pairs) and at session three (post-test) were not statistically significant. None of the session one to three change scores revealed significant differences according to pair type.

We thus have a picture which is strikingly different to that observed with the King and Crown software. Gender differences are attenuated to the point of being almost absent, even with a substantially larger sample size. As before, though, pair type seems to make little difference in itself; the pattern of performance across the three sessions for children who work in mixed sex pairs in session two is very similar to that for children who work in single-sex pairs.

We examined the pattern of mouse control in the mixed-sex pairs on the second session to see whether the pattern of male domination seen with the King and Crown software would be replicated here. It was not. In fact the mean proportion of time the girls controlled the mouse (57 per cent) was significantly greater than that for which the boys controlled the mouse (32 per cent). It being the second session, the children knew what the task was going to be before they sat down. There was no sign at all of the boys ending up sitting on the side which gave them 'dominant hand' access to the mouse; seating positions in the mixed-sex pairs were independent of gender.

The results of the two studies discussed thus far seem to suggest that superficial gender stereotyping of the scenario within which a task is presented may make a very substantial difference to the relative responses of boys and girls. While it should not, perhaps, be surprising that superficial features of the software will have some effect, it also needs to be remembered that many of the explanations put forward to account for gender differences in relation to computers point to longer term factors.

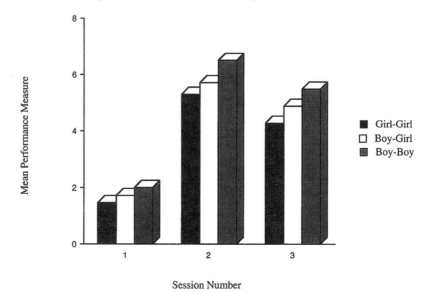

Figure 5.3 The mean level of performance for the three different pair types

Thus, if gender differences are accounted for by differences in cognitive style, preferred ways of working, or histories of exclusion, it should surprise us that they turn out to be so labile.

However, though the difference between the versions of the software in use is the obvious candidate to explain the differing outcomes of these two studies, it is by no means the only possible one. The studies differed in design in a number of ways, such as the inclusion of an individual pre-test in the Honeybears study. Also, the fact that the individual condition in the Honeybears study involved children working at separate machines in the same room rather than on their own might be important. There is some evidence that girls are more disadvantaged than boys by having to work entirely on their own (Whitelock et al., 1993). Thus in order to establish whether it was indeed the version of the software that was making the difference, it was necessary to conduct some further studies (Littleton, Light, Joiner, Messer and Barnes, 1998).

The software contrast studies

The first software contrast study used the King and Crown and Honeybears versions of the software described in the previous chapter and used in the two studies just described. The design was very simple. We took fifty-two children, aged eleven, half boys and half girls. Half the boys and half the girls were randomly allocated in advance to each version of the task. The children were withdrawn from the class in groups of four (two boys and two girls) and they went to a room in which there were four computers. The two boys sat at one machine to start with, and were introduced to one version of the task. They then moved to separate machines and worked on that version of the task on their own. The two girls, meanwhile, were introduced to the other version of the task by a second adult, and went on to work on this version on their own. One of the adult experimenters was male, the other female, and they balanced their roles with respect both to the gender of the children and the version of the software they were working with.

In the initial briefing the children were given a tightly scripted tutorial introduction in which they were shown the goal of the task. They were also shown how to retrieve the information available in the software, how to make a move, and the consequences of attempting to make an impossible move. Finally, the children were informed of the time available (thirty minutes), but told not to worry if they did not solve the problem.

Figure 5.4 shows the average scores for the two gender groupings and two versions of the task. Overall, performance was significantly better on the Honeybears than on the King and Crown version, but there was no significant effect of gender. However, while the performance of the boys remained virtually unaffected by the software type, the performance of the girls was far superior when using the Honeybears software, resulting in a significant interaction effect. Indeed, the girls' mean level of performance on Honeybears slightly exceeded that of the boys, although this difference is not statistically significant.

The results clearly suggest that the performance of the girls was strongly influenced by the version of the task employed. However, the study suffered two weaknesses. Since the Honeybears version of the software was not originally designed to make a comparison with the King and Crown, it differed in a number of ways, for example in the layout of the various screens and the wording of the messages. These differences potentially confound the present comparison. The facilities for automatic computer recording of the children's actions also differed, precluding detailed comparison of the task solution strategies adopted by the children.

To deal with these problems, as well as to see how replicable the previous result would prove, we designed a new version of the King and Crown task called Pirates. This kept the storyline of the King and Crown task, but it shared all design and interface characteristics with Honeybears. Using Pirates and Honeybears as the contrasting versions this time,

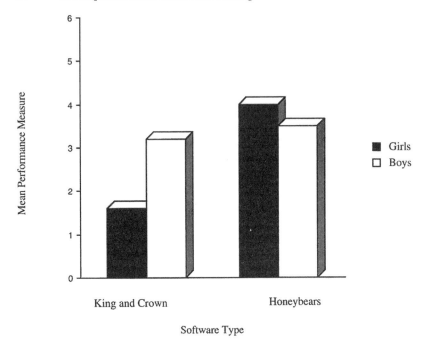

Figure 5.4 The mean level of performance for the girls and boys on the King and Crown and Honeybears versions of the task

we took another sample of eleven year olds (forty-eight this time) and re-ran the study just as before. Half the boys and half the girls were randomly allocated in advance to Pirates and half to Honeybears.

The results are shown in Figure 5.5. This time there was no overall effect of software version, nor was there any overall effect of gender. The interaction between the two, however, remained significant. As before, the boys were apparently little affected by which version of the task they encountered, whereas the girls did far better with the Honeybears version. On average, the girls outperformed the boys on Honeybears, though this difference was not statistically significant.

Inspection of the computer traces showed no significant effect of gender or software type, nor any interaction between these, in terms of how long it took the children to get started on the task, how much information they searched before beginning to make moves, or in the direction of initial moves. The only gender by software interaction discovered from the trace concerned errors associated with the characters in the scenario. Such errors might arise, for example, when a child failed to

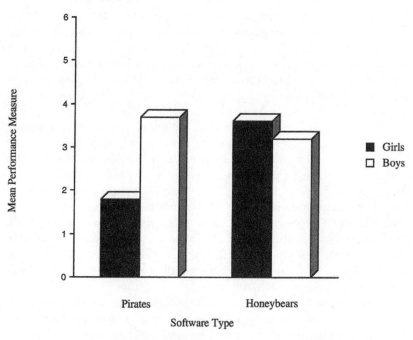

Figure 5.5 The mean level of performance for the girls and boys on the Pirates and Honeybears versions of the task

specify which characters to take on a given move, or specified characters not present at that location. With the Pirates version, girls made more such errors than boys, whereas the reverse was the case for Honeybears.

More generally, it was apparent that many of the girls identified with the characters, and afterwards, for example, some of them spontaneously talked about which bear was their favourite. More than one talked about taking particular bears on their journey to get the honey because 'they wouldn't want to be left behind'. Such personification of the characters was not apparent amongst the boys, or with the King and Crown version. In itself, identification with the characters will not help to solve the task; indeed, it could potentially hinder solution. However, it seems possible that this factor may have affected the girls' motivation to engage with the task.

Taken together, the results of these two software contrast studies show boys' performance to be very little affected by the version of the software they were using. The girls' performance, on the other hand, was very substantially affected by the version of the software they encountered. While the King and Crown and Pirates tasks were not designed to appeal particularly to boys, the roles of the characters were stereotypically masculine ones and the means of transport (cars, ships and planes) had masculine associations. The Honeybears version was designed to be free of these male stereotyped elements; the characters had no explicit gender, and the transports (pony, rowing boats and balloon) were less mechanical. Nonetheless, the underlying task was exactly the same for both versions.

It is possible that the relatively high lability of girls' performance is a function of lower experience/confidence with computers rather than of gender as such. Robinson-Staveley and Cooper (1990) found with older women students that the performance of women with low familiarity and confidence with computers is greatly affected by subtle manipulations of their expectations about how well they will do, whereas women with higher levels of experience of computers are largely unaffected by such manipulations. Unfortunately we do not have independent evidence with the present samples of whether the boys were generally more experienced and confident with computers than the girls, but other research mentioned earlier suggests that this is likely.

These two software contrast studies offer an important message to those involved in designing or choosing software for children's use. Political correctness may be out of fashion, but here there is clear evidence that unthinking gender stereotyping of computer-based learning materials really can make a difference to children's learning. Given an initial motivation to engage with the task, the girls were adept at handling the interface and thinking their way through the problem. In the following section, though, we want to move on from consideration of software effects to more 'interactive' aspects of the gender agenda. To begin with this will involve a return to the other aspect of gender addressed in the earlier studies, namely the relative success of single-sex as compared to mixed-sex pairings.

Interaction and 'coaction' in mixed gender pairs

In the first section of this chapter, we referred to studies which suggest that boys tend to dominate computer resources, get the best machines, keep girls out, and so on. There is a strong suggestion in the literature that the presence of boys may be deleterious to the performance of girls in this area.

The first King and Crown study, as we have seen, did produce evidence of this kind of domination by boys of the interaction with the computer. On the other hand, even in that study girls in the mixed-sex pairs seemed to gain as much from the interaction session as did girls in girl–girl pairs.

More generally, the evidence that mixed-sex pairs and single-sex pairs are marked by different styles of interaction is much clearer than the evidence that children in mixed-sex pairs perform less well or learn less.

Fitzpatrick (1996), for example, showed in a number of studies that interactional patterns in mixed-sex pairs were characterised by constrained interaction, greater task demarcation and less collaborative talk. However, the girls in these pairs showed no less progress in understanding at post-test than girls who had worked in single-sex pairs. Such results should caution us to recognise that the relationship between interaction and learning is far from straightforward.

We saw in the previous chapter (first and second Honeybears studies; Light *et al.*, 1994) that children tended to perform better on the Honeybears task when another child was present in the room working on a similar task than when they were alone with the experimenter. In those studies the children present were always of the same gender. We went on to consider whether mixed-sex pairing might make a difference even here, where there was not overt interaction (we called this a 'coaction' condition).

Sixty-two eleven-year-old children participated in our first study of this issue (Light, Littleton, Bale, Messer and Joiner, in press). The children were assigned at random to ten boy–boy pairs, ten girl–girl pairs and eleven mixed-sex pairs. They were taken in their assigned pairs from their classroom to another room in the school by an unfamiliar (male) experimenter, who gave a brief introduction and demonstration of the Honeybears task and then sat each of them at a computer. The children were told that they probably would not finish the task before the end of the session, but that they should see how far they could get.

The two computers were close to one another, but arranged so that the children could not see one another's screens. They could see one another's faces, but were asked not to talk to one another during the twenty minutes they spent working on the task. The adult remained present throughout the session, but did not intervene in any way. The study involved only a single session for each child.

Figure 5.6 shows the pattern of performance. Boys did slightly better than girls overall, but more interestingly there was a significant gender by pair type interaction. Boys tended to do better when their 'partner' was a girl, but girls tended to do less well when their 'partner' was a boy. The trace data reveal similar statistical interactions in respect of information searching. Girls in mixed-sex pairs spend less time searching for information (both before the first move and overall) than girls in single-sex pairs, whereas the boys spent more time in information searching than boys in single-sex pairs. Thus it seems that in the mixed-sex pairings, the boys are

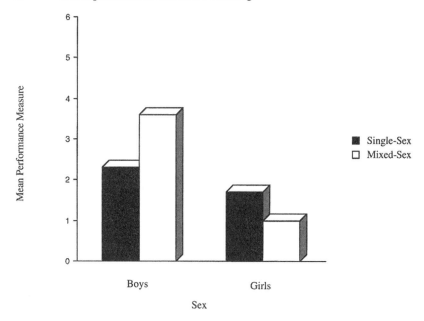

Figure 5.6 The mean level of performance for the mixed and single-sex dyads

behaving *more* planfully, but the girls *less* planfully than in single-sex pairings.

The surprising feature of these results is that, whereas in previous studies children in mixed-sex pairs actually performed at very much the same level as those in single-sex pairs, here we are seeing a significant effect of pair type on performance. But in this case, unlike those which have gone before, the children are not working collaboratively at all, but simply working in proximity with one another. Thus despite evidence that in interactive mixed-sex pairs the boys do indeed tend to dominate the interaction with the computer, we find clearer evidence for the effect of partner gender on performance when partners do not interact around the task than when they do.

On a post-experiment questionnaire, the children were asked whether they thought boys or girls were most interested in, and better at using, computers, or whether they thought both were equal. About half of the children (boys and girls equally) thought that boys were more interested in computers than girls, whereas no child thought the opposite. Only about one third of the children (boys and girls equally) thought that boys were better at using computers than girls, but again no child thought the opposite. Thus we can say that between a third and a half of the children did associate enthusiasm for, and expertise with, computers more with boys than with girls. It seems a fair assumption that this perception has a good deal to do with the observed effects of partner gender on performance.

Before attempting to unpick this further, we decided to conduct a larger study which would allow direct comparison of 'interactive' and 'coactive' mixed-sex pairings. Instead of a single session study, we used a full three stage design, with pre-test and post-test separated by a longer (forty minute) session in which the children worked in pairs either interactively or coactively.

In the first ('pre-test') phase, ninety-six eleven-year-old children were withdrawn from class in single-sex pairs from their classroom by a female experimenter. After a brief, scripted introduction, each of the children worked separately at a computer for ten minutes on a further variant of the problem-solving software called 'Princesses' (in which three princesses have to retrieve the queen's crown, avoiding a sea-witch).

On the basis of their performance on this pre-test, the children were assigned to groups and conditions. All pairs comprised children from different classes in the same school who had the same pre-test score. By taking children from different classes we hoped to minimise the specific prior knowledge they would have of one another's interests and abilities. Half of the children (eight boy–boy pairs, eight girl–girl pairs and eight girl–boy pairs were assigned to the interactive condition. The other half were assigned to the coactive condition. All sub-groups were balanced in terms of mean pre-test scores.

A week after the pre-tests, the children were brought to the testing room with their assigned partner, and given an introduction to the Honeybears version of the task. They were told that they would have forty minutes to work on the task, but not to worry too much about getting it finished because they would have another go on their own the following week.

The children in the interactive condition were seated at a single computer, and were encouraged to share the mouse and to help each other. The children in the coactive condition each sat at their own computer, the screens arranged so that they could not see each other's, and they were asked not to talk to each other during the session. The fifteen-minute post-test session a week later ran just as the pre-test, using Honeybears, but with alterations to some locations so that the children had to 're-solve' the problem rather than just reproducing a remembered sequence of moves.

Since the pairs and sub-groups were all balanced in terms of pre-test scores, the results can be given simply in terms of performance at post-test. Figure 5.7 shows the outcome for the interaction condition. There is no overall sex difference, nor, more importantly for present purposes, is

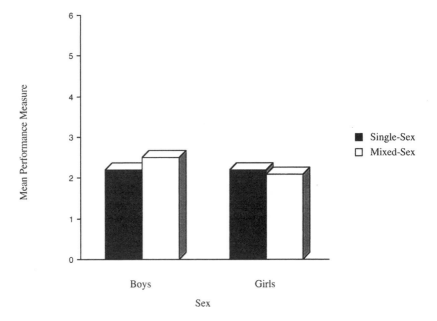

Figure 5.7 The mean level of performance for the mixed and single-sex pairs for the interacting pairs

there any difference as a function of sex of partner. Children who have worked interactively with an opposite-sex partner perform in just the same way at post-test as children who have interacted with a same-sex partner. This replicates our previous findings with interactive pairs.

Figure 5.8 shows the outcome for the coaction condition. We see the same gender polarisation in the mixed gender dyads that we saw in the study just described, reflected once again as a statistically significant interaction. Girls who had worked in the presence of a boy in the practice session did less well at post-test than those who had worked in the presence of another girl. Boys who had worked in the presence of a girl did better than those who had worked in the presence of another boy.

The children's reponses to the question posed after the first of these studies confirmed the general finding that a substantial proportion of the children (both boys and girls) expect boys to be better with computers than girls. Actually, as we have seen over a series of studies with the Honeybears task, there is little or no difference in the average performance of boys and girls. Indeed, in the study just described, pre-test scores were used to create matched pairs, so that the girls and boys were equal in terms of initial ability on the task.

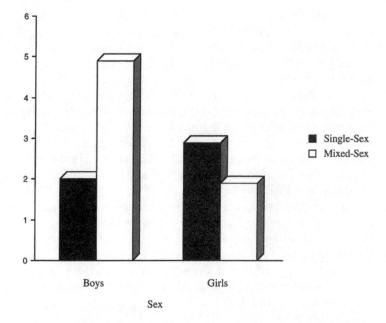

Figure 5.8 The mean level of performance for the mixed and single-sex pairs for the coacting pairs

Where the children work collaboratively, as in the interaction condition, they will have every opportunity to discover each other's competencies and incompetences. This might well result in a defusing of any gender-stereotyped expectations they may have had. In fact, as we saw in studies reported earlier in this chapter, the girls may actually dominate the interaction, at least in terms of executive control of the computer.

Where the children were working in close proximity but without interaction, as in the coaction condition, they did not have the same opportunity to defuse any gendered expectations that they might have brought to the situation. They were kept very much aware of one another's presence; they could see each other whenever they looked up, and could hear the 'beeping' of one another's machines in response to keyboard entries. These noises were not informative as to the partner's progress, but they may well have expected that their relative degrees of success on the task would become evident as the session went on. In fact this was not the case unless one of them completed the task inside the session time, which was infrequent.

It seems plausible to suppose, then, that in the mixed-sex situation the boys were particularly challenged to achieve well, while girls may have been inhibited by seeing themselves to be at a disadvantage from the outset. This explanation links gendered perceptions of relative competence to the effects observed. In this connection, mention should be made of one last Honeybears study, which, unlike the others, drew boys and girls from independent single-sex schools (Flynn, 1995).

The children were aged ten to eleven, and had been privately educated in single-sex preparatory schools for most or all of their schooling. Gender stereotyping in relation to the curriculum is reported to be much less pronounced in single-sex as against mixed-sex schools (Bone, 1983), and indeed it transpired that these children showed no significant sex difference in enthusiasm for computers as indexed by a standard questionnaire (Todman and File, 1990).

Ten boy–boy pairs, ten girl–boy pairs and ten girl–girl pairs were established at random, drawing from two schools. They were given a single twenty minute session on Honeybears, working 'coactively' at two computers. There was no trace of the gender polarisation in the mixed-sex pairs that we had seen in the previous studies. Both the girls and the boys in the mixed-sex pairs behaved as the boy members of such pairs had done in the first of the studies described in this section, that is, they spent significantly more time on information searching than did children in the single-sex pairs.

Overview

In the introduction to this chapter we provided a brief review of the now quite extensive research literature focusing on gender difference in response to computers. Such gender differences are all seen as working to the disadvantage of girls. The pattern of gender difference observed with our King and Crown task seemed to confirm the gloomy picture; the boys dominated the mixed-sex interactions and performed significantly better than the girls on the task at post-test. Nonetheless, it is important to note that the extent of the gender difference in performance was independent of whether the children had worked in same-sex or mixed-sex pairs.

The introduction of the Honeybears version of the task was marked by a striking reduction in both the gender difference in performance and the dominance of the computer interface by the boys. Controlled contrasts of the two versions of the task showed quite clearly that, even with exactly the same underlying task, the setting of the task made a great deal of difference to the performance of the girls. The gender difference which was so striking in the King and Crown task could be ameliorated or indeed eliminated by simply altering the storyline and characters involved. Whether versions of the task could be found which create significant performance advantages for the girls remains to be seen, but the evidence presented here seems sufficient to merit the close attention of those involved in educational software development and selection.

The software contrast studies strongly suggest that there is nothing immutable about gender differences in this area. The results with mixed-sex pairs in interaction around the computer suggest that even where there is apparently a high degree of dominance, the relationship to learning outcomes is by no means straightforward. The final studies described in this chapter contrasted mixed-sex pairs in interaction with mixed-sex pairs whose members were simply 'coacting': working on separate computers without (overt) interaction. The degree of gender polarisation of performance was stronger in the latter case than in the former.

Our tentative interpretation is that it is not gender so much as self-confidence that is at issue. This interpretation finds some support in a study by Robinson-Staveley and Cooper (1990), mentioned earlier. When expectation of success on a computer task was artificially manipulated, both male and female students with low induced expectancy of success were impaired by the presence of someone else, while those with high induced expectations performed better in the presence of someone else than when alone.

Some further evidence comes from a quite separate study using a computer based mathematical reasoning task (Joiner, Messer, Steele, Light and Littleton, 1993). In this study, again with children aged ten and eleven, we found that the performance of children with high computer experience was facilitated by the presence of others working on the same task, whereas the performance of children with low computer experience was inhibited by the presence of others, both in terms of the time taken and the number of problems successfully solved.

An interesting finding relating directly to software contrasts is reported by Cooper, Hall and Huff (1990). Their study was based upon a comparison of maths software with very masculine imagery (called 'Demolition division', involving tanks etc.) with a comparable maths package without any such aggressive imagery. The children (twelve- to fourteen-year-olds) completed an anxiety inventory after working on one or other type of software. When working in mixed gender 'coactive' grouping of sixteen in the school computer room, the girls reported higher levels of anxiety after working with the 'aggressive' software than with the other, and the reverse was true for the boys. This interaction between the sex of the child and the software type was not found when the children used the software on their own, in privacy.

Unfortunately, Cooper et al.'s study did not include performance measures for both types of software, and their demands were in any case not directly comparable. Nonetheless, their conclusion that: 'Gender biased software is a stressor to the opposite sex if it is encountered in the presence of observers or possible observers' (1990, p. 426) is relevant to interpreting the present results.

Overall, the conclusion to be drawn from the studies reported in this chapter must be that the effectiveness of peer interaction in learning situations may be as much a matter of social comparison as it is of social interaction. The focus of both Piagetian and Vygotskian work in this field has been on identifying the cognitively constructive elements of interaction. The results discussed here suggest that a more social-psychological approach, focusing on children's perceptions of their own ability relative to the task and to their partner, may be at least as illuminating. Thus we are pushed from an interpretation of peer facilitation effects in terms of observable, cognitively productive forms of interaction towards a recognition that at least some of the effects may depend on less directly observable social processes. These will be the focus of the next chapter.

6   Social comparison and learning

Social comparison and 'social loafing'

The study of processes of social comparison has been central to social psychology but marginal to developmental psychology. However, as we have seen in the last two chapters, results of peer interaction studies seem to force issues of social comparison to our attention. This chapter begins with a brief overview of some of the relevant background literature, with a particular focus on recent research by Monteil, Huguet and colleagues in France. We shall then introduce further empirical studies which build upon Monteil's work as well as our own.

Social comparison processes bridge the gap between issues of self and the sense of personal identity on the one hand, and of interpersonal and intergroup processes on the other. At its baldest, the term social comparison simply refers to any comparison an individual might make between his or her own attributes or abilities with those of someone else. Festinger (1954) highlighted the power of social comparisons in situations where individuals have no firm objective criterion by which to judge themselves or their performance. Many of the judgements we make about ourselves are relative, and may fluctuate according to who else is available to compare ourselves with (Durkin, 1995; Gergen, 1977).

The role of social comparison processes in socialisation (in the acquisition of norms and evaluation of the self against those norms) has been the subject of some developmental research (Ruble, 1983). Seven to eleven year olds given repeated sessions on a mathematics task were found by Ruble and Flett (1988) to pay more attention to comparisons of their own performance to that of peers than to comparisons of their own present and previous performance, though the more able older children did show greater interest in the latter type of comparison. Durkin (1995) suggests that with development, individuals make more and more selective comparisons, based on such things as perceived similarity and common group membership.

Social comparisons begin early in life, but it appears that comparisons of ability figure prominently in children's thinking only from about the age of seven (Ruble and Frey, 1991). It is difficult to be sure how far schooling, as opposed to age, might be responsible here. There is some evidence that social context can make a significant difference. For example, seven- and eight-year-old Israeli children raised in kibbutzim are less likely to think in terms of competitive, ability-based comparisons than their urban peers are (Butler and Ruzany, 1993).

Social comparison effects in school contexts are particularly relevant for present purposes. Marshall and Weinstein (1984) showed that a variety of contextual factors could make a difference to the way social comparison factors affected school performance, notably the 'visibility' of the social comparisons themselves. The effects of performance-related feedback, for example, differed according to whether that feedback was delivered to the children privately or in front of the group. Not surprisingly, it appears that cooperative working arrangements weaken the focus on social comparisons of individual ability, whereas competitive working arrangements heighten the salience of such comparisons (Ames, 1981).

A considerable body of research on the effects of evaluative feedback on performance indicates that such effects are most frequently positive, but sometimes negative (Kluger and DeNisi, 1996). Monteil and Huguet (in press) believe that the apparently inconsistent results can be explained if attention is given to the circumstances of feedback. In particular, the key, as they see it, is whether feedback on performance is given in circumstances which place the child in a situation of social comparison with another.

Monteil and Huguet have returned to some of the earliest studies of social facilitation of learning to try to establish a role for social comparison. Triplett (1898) is widely cited as offering a clear demonstration that, for children aged nine to thirteen, the presence of another child working on the same task (a simple motor skill task) facilitated performance. Actually, according to Monteil and Huguet, a quarter of Triplett's participants showed no effect and another quarter showed a negative (inhibitory) effect of peer presence.

Burnham (1905) compared the performance of children in classes at school with the performance of children working alone at home, and concluded that performance in class was superior for activities which did not demand much originality, but the opposite was true for more creative tasks. Much later, Zajonc (1965) also offered evidence which seemed to point to a task effect, namely that peer presence is facilitatory with simple tasks but inhibitory with complex tasks.

Zajonc offered an account of his results in terms of an essentially behaviourist 'drive theory', according to which the presence of others raised the level of general drive, and favoured the production of the most readily available response to the task in hand. With simple tasks, this response is likely to be correct, so that performance facilitation results. With more complex tasks, successful solution may depend on the inhibition of such dominant responses, and raised levels of general drive may thus reduce the quality of performance.

Cottrell, Wack, Sekerak and Rittle (1968) argued that it was not so much the mere presence of individuals that makes a difference, but rather the 'evaluation potential' of the audience. They showed, for example, that for individuals performing a task, the presence of others made no difference if they were blindfolded, but it did make a difference if they were watching the performance keenly.

Both the pattern of findings reported by Zajonc and his approach to explaining them have found mixed support in subsequent research (Bond and Titus, 1983; Glaser, 1982). The predicted pattern of results for simple and complex tasks does not always occur, especially in relation to tasks involving memory and cognition (Hartwick and Nagao, 1990).

There have been a number of attempts to reconceptualise the issue of social facilitation in more cognitive terms. For example, Manstead and Semin (1980) argued that the presence of the other could be seen as making demands on finite attentional resources, to the detriment of learning tasks calling for considerable attention. 'Automated' performances, on the other hand, demand little attention and may benefit from anything which maintains alertness.

This focus on attentional resources and their disposition underpins the approach of Monteil and Huguet (in press), who report an unpublished study in which Huguet, Monteil and Galvaing used the Stroop test to try to distinguish dominant response explanations from explanations based on attention. With, for example, the word (e.g. 'red') written in a different colour (e.g. green), the participant is asked to name the colour. The correct answer is thus 'green', but the interfering dominant response (to read the word) will tend to generate the erroneous response 'red'.

In these circumstances, if the presence of another person increases the tendency to generate the dominant response it should lead to a decrement in performance. However, if the presence of another person makes it harder to focus attention, as Monteil and Huguet suppose, then it might be expected to improve performance. The results showed that provided the other person was attentive and looking at the participant, Stroop interference was reduced and performance improved.

But Monteil and Huguet are seeking to foster a position which is not only more cognitively oriented than Zajonc's, but also more socially oriented. They emphasise the importance of the participant's personal perspective on the task and the broader situation within which it is set. Participants come to learning situations with a history of experience of their performance across a range of more or less related tasks in more or less related situations; an 'autobiography' of themselves as learners. The central point here is that the presence of another can generate different significations according to the history of the individual learner. Social contexts do not exist independently of the individual. Rather: 'Social contexts exist only through the intervention of cognitive structures of contextualisation, such as those linked to the autobiographical memory of the individual' (Monteil and Huguet, in press). In other words, while individual performance depends upon social contexts, social contexts can only be understood in terms of individuals.

Monteil and Huguet (in press) point out that a number of studies over the last twenty years or so have suggested that the experience of the individual immediately prior to the peer presence situation can make a significant difference to the outcome observed. For example, Mash and Hedley (1975) showed that a positive interchange with the experimenter led to facilitative effects of subsequent peer presence on a simple motor task, but a negative interchange with the experimenter resulted in inhibitory effects of subsequent peer presence. Similarly, Seta and Hassan (1980) showed that audience effects could vary according to the individual's immediately prior history of success and failure on the task. Using a memory task, they showed that the presence of an audience improved the performance of those with a previous history of success but impaired that of those who had encountered failure.

If social comparison is one key concept in twentieth century social psychology, 'social loafing' is another. Ringelmann (1913) observed that the total physical effort produced by a group (in response to a task involving pulling on a rope) was less than the sum of the effort put in if each member of the group worked alone. The difference was found to be proportional to the size of the group. The term 'social loafing' was subsequently introduced to refer to the tendency of individuals to produce less effort in group than in individual situations. It has been shown that social loafing does not occur in a situation where the individual contributions of the participants are expected to be identifiable (Williams, Harkins and Latane, 1981). It seems that evaluation (or the potential for evaluation) of relative performance is a determining factor in this regard.

Monteil and Huguet (in press) are critical of research in this area because of its characteristic neglect of the history of experience of the individual participant. They cite a study by Sanna (1992) in which individuals were paired for a vigilance task. Having received feedback indicating that they were doing better or worse than their partner, they went on either to work as a pair (where their success would be judged on 'group product') or coactively (where their individual success levels would be visible). Those who had been favoured by the initial comparison subsequently performed better in the coaction than the group condition (a result consistent with social loafing). However, the reverse was true of those whose initial feedback had suggested that they were doing less well.

It seems, then, that social comparisons can moderate the effects attributed to social loafing. So too can individual differences of a more general/stable kind. Huguet, Charbonnier and Monteil (1995) showed that reduced productivity in a collective as against a coactive situation was characteristic only of students who were high on 'self-uniqueness', as indexed by a separately administered questionnaire. Extending this to cultural differences, Gabrenya, Wang and Latane (1985) have shown in a comparison of Chinese and North American students that social loafing was characteristic only of North American males. Chinese males showed exactly the opposite pattern ('social striving'). Without wanting here to open up the complex debate about individualistic and collectivist cultures, we can simply recognise that universal accounts which take no account of individual, social and cultural characteristics are unlikely to be adequate to the phenomena. For example, social loafing appears to be more a male than a female phenomenon: Karau and Williams, 1993, and Monteil and Huguet, in press, report data indicating that while boys produce better memory recall performance in 'public' than in anonymous conditions, the reverse is true for girls.

Social comparison and children's learning

Monteil (1988) describes a series of studies which attest to the subtle interaction of individual abilities, personal histories and social contexts for learning. In his first study, participants were fourteen- and fifteen-year-olds, selected as having either high or low levels of general educational attainment. The children were placed in groups of eight (four high performers and four low in each group). Then, in the 'Social comparison' condition, the children were publicly told their actual educational levels. In the 'No social comparison' condition they were told that they were all at the same (unspecified) level. They were then taught some biology in a forty-five minute lesson, either in a 'individuated' condition (where they were told to expect to be questioned individually during the lesson), or in an 'anonymous' condition (where they knew that they would not be singled out for questioning). No questioning actually occurred in either condition, but after the lesson all students completed a written test on the material taught.

In the 'No social comparison' condition, the high attainers did better on the test than the low attainers, and the individuation/anonymity manipulation had no effect. In the 'Social comparison' condition, however, individuation led to an amplification of the difference between the high and low attainers, while anonymity reduced the difference to almost nothing. Given the combination of social comparison and anonymity, the high attaining pupils did rather less well than they had done in other situations, while the low attainers did exceptionally well.

Similar results were obtained in a second study conducted with only high attaining pupils. Here, social comparisons were introduced by giving pupils feedback on a prior task, indicating success or failure. Even when this feedback was actually uncorrelated with real performance, it engendered the same pattern of results. Negative feedback was followed by better learning under anonymous than under individuated conditions, while positive feedback was followed by better performance under individuated than under anonymous conditions (Monteil, 1988).

Subsequent studies showed that the effects shown in these initial studies are also conditioned by the academic context in which the task is set, being evident for highly valued disciplines such as mathematics and biology, but not for lower valued disciplines such as 'technical and manual education'. This observation opened up a new line of research, in which Monteil and Huguet (1991) explored the effects of representing a given standard task to some students as 'geometry' and to others as 'drawing'. The actual task was always the same and involved a complex rectilinear figure (see Figure. 6.1), which the pupils were shown for a short period of time and asked to remember. Their success on both a recall (which involved drawing from memory) and a recognition task was shown to vary as a function of both discipline context and their own academic standing. When the task was represented as being 'geometry', there was a large difference in memory performance between the children classed as generally high attainers and those classed as low attainers, with the high attainers doing better. However, when the task was represented as 'drawing' there was no difference in performance between the two groups.

This intriguing result prompted us to attempt a replication in the UK. It seemed possible that the results reported by Monteil and Huguet might depend upon certain features of the French education system which differentiated it from the British system. In particular, it appears that pupils are made more explicitly aware of their own levels of academic performance in France than in the UK. For example, they are required to

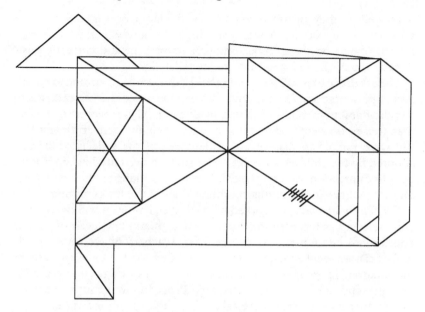

Figure 6.1 The complex rectilinear figure

repeat an academic year if they fail to reach a certain standard. Similarly, it seemed to us possible that the high valuation of some disciplines (especially mathematics) might be more characteristic of French than of British schools.

For reasons of convenience, we worked with children of middle school age (eleven- and twelve-year-olds) rather than the somewhat older secondary pupils used by Monteil and Huguet. We used the terms 'maths' and 'art' (in place of 'geometry' and 'drawing') in relation to the same rectilinear figure illustrated in Figure 6.1 (Light, 1994; Littleton, Light, Robertson and Beeton, in preparation).

A pilot study involved the presentation of the memory task to fifty-two children, unselected for ability, to see whether the representation of the task as maths or drawing made a significant difference for British children of this age level. The children were taken from their classes in groups of four and were told that we were doing a survey in different schools of how well children of their age could do in different subjects. Half of the groups were then told that they had been chosen for a maths test and the other half that they had been chosen for an art test. Each child, working individually, was presented with the figure on paper to look at for one minute. They were then given a pencil and paper and asked to reproduce it as well as they possibly could, as a freehand drawing. Scoring of accuracy of reproduction was done blind by judges, using a scoring system (based on the number of elements present and correctly positioned) which showed good interjudge reliability.

The accuracy of recall scores did show a difference according to condition of presentation. The children who had been told that the task was to test their ability in maths obtained significantly higher scores (mean 22) than those who were told that it was to test their ability in art (mean 17). We were unable to discern any differences in the style or technique adopted by the children working under the two presentation conditions, but our impression was that the children were working on their reproductions for longer in the maths condition than in the art condition.

For the main study we worked with forty-eight eleven and twelve year olds, selected as representing particularly high and low levels of general educational attainment. At our request, teachers of six state middle school classes selected the two *highest* attaining and the two *lowest* attaining children of each sex from their class, giving us twenty-four high attainers and twenty-four low attainers. Procedure was much as before, except that the children were taken from their class individually. On arrival in the testing room, they were told that they were taking part in a survey, as in the previous study. However, before they were told which subject they were going to be tested in they were asked to rank nine school subjects in terms of how important they were, and then in terms of how good they thought they were at each. After this, half of them were told that they were going to take part in a maths test, the other half that they were going to take part in an art test.

Procedure was then as before, except that while they worked on reproducing the figure they were timed, and they were asked to stop when they could not remember any more. The pattern of results echoed that observed by Monteil and Huguet (1991), in that the high attainers produced significantly better recall performance when they were told that it was a maths test (mean score 23) than when they were told that it was an art test (mean 19). The reverse was true for the low attainers (mean 13 for maths, 15 for art), though this difference was nonsignificant.

The same pattern was true to a more marked degree in respect of the time spent by the children working on their reproduction of the figure. High attainers tended to be quicker overall, but spent more time on recall in the maths condition (mean 121 secs) than in the art condition (mean 115 secs). By contrast, low attainers spent more time on recall in the art condition (mean 143 secs) than in the maths condition (mean 115 secs). This resulted in a statistically significant interaction between attainment level and presentation condition.

For the high attainers, the modal ranking of importance for maths was 1 (i.e. it was seen as the most important subject of the nine subjects listed). For the low attainers the modal ranking of the importance of maths was significantly lower, at sixth in the list of nine. However, both high and low attainers put art lower down the importance ranking than maths, with a modal ranking of 8 from both groups. For the high attainers, maths was seen as significantly more important than art, whereas for the low attainers this difference was not significant.

Overall, the higher the relative importance children attached to the subject in which they were supposedly being tested, the longer they tended to spend on the reproduction of the figure from memory. This relationship did not quite reach a satisfactory level of statistical significance, but again seems to indicate that taking a longer time is indicative of greater effort and attention.

When asked to rank the subjects in terms of how good they thought they were at them, the high attainers gave themselves a modal rank of 2 for maths, whereas the lower attainers gave themselves a modal rank of 9 for maths, indicating that this was the subject they were least good at. However, there was a great deal of individual variability, and this difference was not reliable. For art, however, there was a statistically reliable difference between the rankings the low attainers gave themselves (modal rank 1) and those the high attainers gave themselves (modal rank 9).

Taken together with Monteil and Huguet's earlier findings, these results testify to the extent to which the apparent disciplinary context of a task can make a difference even when the task itself remains exactly the same. The success children have with academic tasks clearly can depend upon how the task is labelled and how the children perceive their own abilities in relation to that label. More generally, the interaction between levels of attainment and disciplinary context shows once again that given contexts depend for their effects upon individual attributes and histories.

In an extension of this work with the memory task, we returned to the question of learning with computers, and to the issue of gender. The figure shown in Figure 6.1 was presented to sixty-four eleven year olds, half of them male, half female. To half of the boys and half of the girls, the figure was presented as before, on paper. To the other half it was presented on a computer screen. In all cases, the children were required simply to look at it, and then to reproduce it from memory on paper. Thus even in the 'computer' condition, the children did not actually have to *do* anything with the computer at all.

Children came to the testing room in same-sex pairs, but worked separately, without interaction and without being able to see what each other were doing. Either both were in the 'computer' condition, or

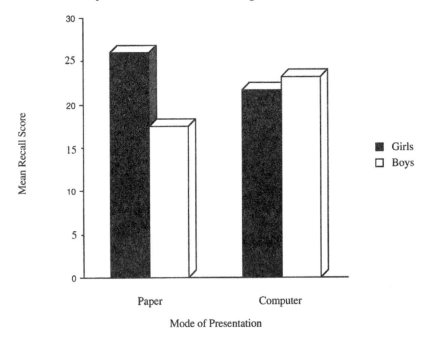

Figure 6.2 The mean recall score for the girls and boys for the two modes of task presentation

neither were. If they were in the 'computer' condition, the task was prefaced by some general questions about whether they enjoyed working with computers, whether they had one at home, and so on.

The pattern of results in terms of recall scores is shown in Figure 6.2. As can be seen, the girls did better when the task was presented on paper than when it was presented on computer, while the reverse was true of the boys. This resulted in a statistically significant interaction between gender and condition effects in an analysis of variance. A simple main effect analysis showed the gender difference in the 'on paper' condition to be statistically significant.

A similar pattern of results was shown in terms of a different test of memory, which involved recognition. This was done after the recall task, and involved pupils being presented with a series of twenty paired images. Members of each pair were identical except in orientation. Children had to decide whether the image represented a fragment of the original figure or not, and if so, which image was correctly oriented.

For children in the 'on paper' condition, the paired images were presented as a booklet, with a pair of images on each page. For children

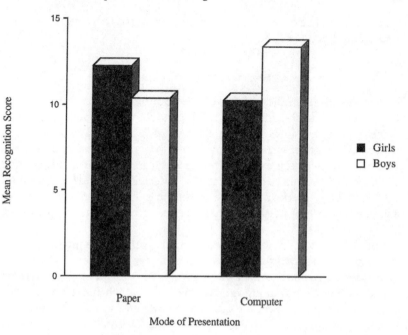

Figure 6.3 The mean recognition score for the girls and boys for the two modes of task presentation

in the 'computer' condition the images were presented on the computer screen and the children used specified keys on the keyboard to make their responses. Figure 6.3 shows the results; there was a significant interaction between gender and condition. Girls tended to show better recognition scores when the task was presented on paper, but boys scored significantly better than girls when the task was presented on computer.

Direct comparisons of the same task undertaken on and off computer are surprisingly few and far between, so it may be appropriate here to mention briefly an unpublished study (Humphreys, 1995) which looked at the performance of boys and girls on physical and computer screen versions of the Tower of Hanoi problem described in Chapter 2. Eighty children, aged ten and eleven, working in coactive pairs (i.e. without interaction) attempted the Tower of Hanoi task either as a wooden puzzle or on the screen. While boys and girls took approximately the same time to complete the physical version of the task, boys were significantly quicker on the screen version than girls were, resulting in a statistically significant interaction. However, the same pattern was not shown for the numbers of moves needed to complete the task; here there was no significant effect of gender.

Game versus test context

As well as these studies of how far computer presentation of a task influenced responses differentially by gender, we designed a study to address the question of how *far the context in which a computer task* is presented can affect girls' and boys' on-task performance. In an experimental study involving sixty children aged ten and eleven (thirty boys and thirty girls), we examined the effects of differential contextualisation on girls' and boys' performance on a computer-based perceptual-motor skills task (Littleton, Ashman, Light, Artis, Roberts and Oosterwegel, 1999).

The task was a specially designed computer version of a physical device in which the participant attempts to guide a wire ring around a bent wire frame without making contact with the wire. The screen version consisted of a double cursor framing an irregular line, which moved across the screen at a regular speed. Figure 6.4 shows the starting set up as it appeared to the child. Note that the window labels could be changed so as to display a stereotypically masculine label (technician's skills test), a stereotypically feminine label (beautician's skills test) or a game label (electric eel game) as appropriate.

The line moved from right to left across the screen. The objective was to use the mouse in order to raise and lower the cursor in such a way that the line would pass smoothly through the gap, without hitting the cursor 'ring'. If there was contact, a beep sounded and the line stopped until the cursor was moved so as to free up the line again.

Each child was seen individually in a quiet side room in the school. The task, with one of the possible labels, was loaded on the screen before the child came in. After the child had been seated in front of the computer, the experimenter sat to one side of the computer and gave a scripted introduction. For example, in the case of the feminine context the instructions were as follows: 'I'm interested to see how children of your age get along with some computer programs. I'm trying out a few different things today. The one I'd like you to do is designed as a test to see how good people will be as beauticians.' The ending of this introduction was amended according to the experimental condition. In the case of the masculine context the children were told that the program was 'designed as a test to see how good people will be as technicians'. In the case of the game context, the children were told that the program was 'designed as a computer game and is called electric eel.'

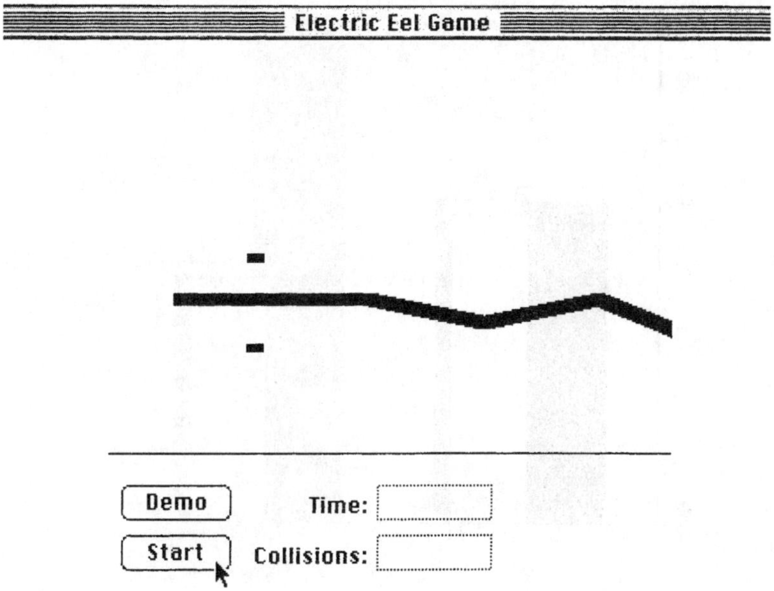

Electric Eel Game

Figure 6.4 The perceptual-motor skills task

The experimenter then ran a ten second demonstration during which she controlled the mouse and described the task. The children then ran the demonstration for themselves as a practice session. Just as each child began to embark upon the session from which their performance data were derived, the experimenter reinforced the context by saying 'OK, now it's your turn to do the beautician's skills test /technician's skills test/ electric eel game.' The experimenter then recorded details of the performance measure, the number of hits incurred, and the screen was then cleared so that the next participant would not see the previous scores.

Analysis of the frequency of 'hits' (i.e. occasions on which the cursor ring was allowed to hit the line) revealed no significant main effects nor any evidence of a significant interaction between gender and context. However, from a closer inspection of means it appeared that heterogeneity of performance within the skills test conditions was potentially masking evidence of gender-related performance differences in the game condition. We thus decided to undertake a further series of post hoc comparisons. These revealed a significant simple main effect of gender in the game context with the performance of the girls being significantly worse (i.e. more hits) than that of the boys. There were no significant gender effects for either of the two skills tests.

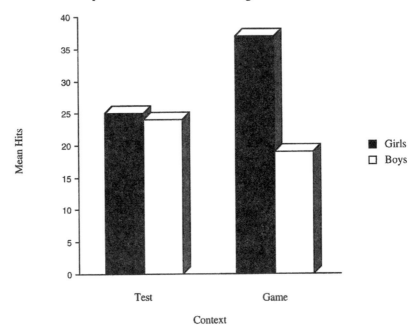

Figure 6.5 The mean 'hits' for the girls and boys in the test and game conditions

The pattern of results thus suggests that the important distinction is not between the beautician or technician contexts but rather between 'game' and 'test' contexts. If the context factor is treated as having only these two levels, the resulting two-factor analysis of variance shows not only that boys do rather better than girls overall, but more interestingly a significant interaction between gender and context (see Figure 6.5).

Further analysis reveals that where the task is introduced as a *test* there is no trace of a performance difference between the girls and the boys. By contrast, when exactly the same task is introduced as a *game* the boys' and girls' performance diverges to a point where there is a significant gender difference in performance favouring the boys. Moreover, the girls performed significantly better when the task was described as a *test* than when it was described as a *game*.

The data suggest that the gendered specification of the 'test' contextualisation (as beautician or technician) had no effect on the performance of girls and boys. More generally the boys' performance appears to be very little affected by the context of the task presentation. This is not a ceiling effect, as there was considerable room for improvement. The girls' performance, on the other hand, was significantly affected by the particular context encountered, deteriorating dramatically in the 'game' context.

In attempting to address the reasons for this it is perhaps worth noting that an answer cannot easily be found within the mainstream cognitive psychology literature. To the archetypal cognitive psychologist, a task is a task is a task. It possesses clear demand characteristics. It can be defined essentially from the outside. Its meaning is determinate. The act of differentially contextualising a task should, from such a point of view, make no difference to a participant's performance on that task. Yet here there is compelling evidence that it can matter considerably. Participants' 'readings' of a task can, in certain circumstances, impact profoundly on their performance on-task.

In terms of explaining our findings, we can offer four possible accounts. All involve the recognition that the interaction between the experimenter, the task and the child is of paramount importance. An experimenter does not simply 'deliver' a set of instructions to a participant. In introducing a task to a participant the experimenter is creating a crucial frame of reference, constructing a context within which the child is enjoined to work. The participant attempts to build an understanding of what is expected and of the intentions and motives of the experimenter, through a process of interpretation and re-interpretation of the experimenter's action and interaction.

As noted above, the interaction between experimenter and participant in an experimental setting is a subtle exercise in 'sense making', which will be shaped in part by the wider cultural context within which the interaction is located. In this particular study the experiment is being conducted within a school setting. Conducting research studies with children in schools undoubtedly affords many distinct advantages, for example, relative ease of access to large numbers of participants. But such an arrangement may have considerable implications for the data which result from such studies. Responses may be determined by a complex contextual system, which extends far beyond the immediate interaction between experimenter and participant, and which is inseparable from the way that education and educational activity is defined in our culture.

We know from the wider educational literature that, as a group, girls tend to be interested in, and sensitive to, the social context of schooling. They are highly skilled at 'making sense of school' and are more motivated than boys are to understand what it means to be a pupil and what it means to 'do' school tasks (Barber, 1994; Davies and Brember, 1995). A first line of explanation of girls' performance in the game context might thus reflect their uncertainty regarding how to read the intentions and motives of an unfamiliar adult who, when working in a classroom setting during lesson time, instructs them to play a computer game. What is the purpose of such activity? The playing of computer games is not part and parcel of recognised daily classroom activity. Thus there is a mismatch between the girls' understanding of what constitutes an appropriate school task and the task they were asked to perform. We might thus speculate that the girls do not know how to make sense of this interaction with the experimenter, that they are unsure as to the purpose and meaning of the activity they have been asked to undertake, since computer gaming has nothing to do with the business of schooling.

Seen in these terms, then, the girls' substantially better performance in the 'test' conditions would reflect the fact that the intentions and motives of the experimenter and the purpose of the activity is less ambiguous and more appropriate to a school context. Although the unfamiliar adult is asking them to perform a computerised vocational skills test, which they would not be familiar with, a test is an activity wholly appropriate to the classroom context. Tests are an integral feature of the school experience. Moreover, adults who are not members of teaching staff (for example, educational psychologists) can often be seen in school administering tests to children.

This account rests on the assumption that girls tend to prefer 'purposeful' activity and that they demonstrate sensitivity to context in a way that boys tend not to. This is an assumption which has some grounding in the wider educational literature. For example, data from the Assessment of Performance Unit in Science reveal that within the domain of science, girls take into account the circumstances within which a task is set, whereas boys, as a group, consider the task in isolation from its context (Murphy, 1993).

A second possible explanation, also predicated on the notion of girls' sensitivity to context, concerns the cultural significations of the context 'game'. There is a vast amount of literature pointing to the significant association between gender and frequency of electronic game playing (Griffiths, 1991). Males tend to have considerably more computer-game experience than females, both in childhood (Subrahmanyam and Greenfield, 1994) and adulthood (Greenfield, Brannon and Lohr, 1994). They have 'learned how to learn' video games and have played and practised on them extensively and enthusiastically. Girls tend not to be enthusiastic game players. For example, when interviewing children about their thoughts on video games Stutz found that the girls were less keen than boys on gaming because they saw the computer world as being biased towards the male perspective and they were therefore discouraged from taking an interest in them (Stutz, 1996). It is therefore possible that the contextualising of the activity as a 'game' effectively categorises the task as an activity somehow more appropriate for boys. Disengagement from the task then leads to a relative decrease in the girls' performance. A variant on this might posit that the description of the task as a game places the girls in a position of relative inexperience and it is an anticipation of failure which becomes a self-fulfilling prophecy.

The further alternative is simply that the girls view the activity of gaming as a frivolous, unimportant activity and that their performance on the task is of little consequence. Aspects of identity are not bound up with being a computer gaming expert. The context of a 'test', on the other hand, may signal the need to try to perform well. Getting good marks on tests in school is bound up with their sense of pupil identity. The lower performance of the girls in the game condition may thus simply reflect the fact that their reading of the task was one where outcome was not particularly important to them. Less good performance is not an indicator of failure, but rather a reflection of a lack of concern.

It would be hard to demonstrate experimentally which of these explanations could best account for the girls' response to the categorisation of the task as a game. Careful post-task interviewing of the female participants could have a role to play here. Unfortunately, such data are not available to us in this study. It may, however, be possible for further studies to distinguish at least the first of the explanations ventured above from the others. The first explanation rests on the notion that encountering a game in a *school* context is particularly problematic. If this is the case, then we should not expect this pattern to be replicated if the same study were to be undertaken in non-school settings.

The present findings resonate with those of other researchers interested in children's interactions with computer technology. For example, Malone (1981) studied the software preferences of school children and discovered that males had a preference for games or toys which provide interactive opportunities simply for their own sake. Girls on the other hand preferred purposeful software which might be classified as tools. Findings such as those reported by Malone and those presented here are of some significance just at the moment, because of the growth of the 'edutainment industry' aimed at both home and school markets. Games are supposed to be synonymous with motivating children to learn and making learning fun. Currently, we hear a good deal about the potential of software with game-like qualities to promote learning (Griffiths, 1996) and computer game formats are increasingly being used as vehicles for educational tasks. The findings reported here suggest that, if we are concerned about fostering girls' enthusiasm for computers, then the presentation of a task as a *game* may be a hindrance to, rather than a support for, learning and engagement.

Overview

The results of these various studies show that, quite independently of the intrinsic difficulty of the tasks concerned, presenting a task on a computer can make a difference to performance. Not only that, but computer presentation has a *differential* impact on the performance of girls and boys. As the first result in this section showed, this differential effect is evident even when the children do not need actually to do anything with the computer at all. We have also seen that variations in the contextualisation of the task also makes a difference as a function of gender. Thus we are dealing here with effects which owe more to individuals' self-perceptions and attributions than to their abilities – if indeed we can still meaningfully separate these. The clear message emerging from this work is that there is a fundamental interrelationship between the cognitive and the social; the social and emotional dimensions of learning are not analytically separate or distinct from the activity of learning. A learning situation is an inextricably social situation. The recognition of this poses considerable methodological and theoretical challenges. How best to study and conceptualise the learner and the activity of learning? Does it make sense to, as we have done in places, appeal to the notion 'ability' or refer to 'high and low achievers' when we have seen that the children's on-task performance is contextually determined? In the final chapter we attempt to address some of these issues.

7   Interaction and learning: rethinking the issues

Talking and learning

The central thesis of this book is that cognitive development and learning are fundamentally social processes. Whilst it is undoubtedly important to consider the role of more experienced cultural actors in promoting development and learning, our own concern has been mainly with the contribution of interaction between peers.

Our earliest investigations of children's collaborative learning and problem solving addressed the issues of whether and when working collaboratively in pairs would prove more effective than working alone. As Chapters 2 and 4 make clear, we soon amassed compelling evidence that in certain circumstances two heads were indeed better than one. This research, which focused primarily on the outcomes and products of collaborative work, was later complemented by a series of studies designed to shed light on the *processes* of collaborative learning. At first our analyses of the talk and joint activity of children were informed by neo-Piagetian conceptions of 'socio-cognitive conflict'. Our primary research question was whether individual progress in understanding could be promoted through exposure to the conflicting ideas of a peer in the context of collaborative problem solving. Whilst the notion of socio-cognitive conflict afforded some explanatory power, it was also apparent that more often than not collaborative gains seemed to have very little to do with 'decentring through conflict' in Doise's sense (Doise, 1990). Rather, progress appeared to be associated with socially mediated processes of conflict *resolution*. The associated concepts of argumentation and negotiation led us to adopt an inherently social model of productive interaction inspired by 'social constructivist' approaches emphasising processes of joint construction of understanding.

Underpinned by conceptual and methodological tools derived from neo-Piagetian and neo-Vygotskian traditions of research, our work has focused primarily on examining the relationship between particular forms of talk and subsequent individual cognition. Our research strategy has been to use correlational techniques to determine whether there is evidence of an association between particular features of the learners' talk (identified using categorical coding schemes) and individual learning gains. In common with many others working in this field, we have treated learning in terms of conceptual accomplishments at an individual level, demonstrable through various forms of post-test. However, in recent years a more radical perspective has been emerging in the research literature on collaboration and learning, a perspective in which social interaction is seen not just as a *stimulus* to individual thinking but as, in effect, 'a social mode of thinking' (Mercer and Wegerif, 1998).

Such a conceptualisation implies that 'talk and social interaction are not just the means by which people learn to think, but also how they engage in thinking . . . discourse *is* cognition *is* discourse . . . One is unimaginable without the other' (Resnick, Pontecorvo and Säljö, 1997, p.2). As Resnick and colleagues recognise, the notion that concepts and ideas are constituted in interactive discourse represents a challenge to traditional accounts of the nature of knowledge. It implies that 'ways of thinking are embedded in ways of using language' (Wegerif and Mercer, 1997, p.51).

This view of cognition challenges our traditional conceptions of development and learning. It invites us to reject a conception of the developmental process as the creation of an autonomous thinker who, through a reconstructive process of internalisation, has acquired the resources and tools of a culture (Packer, 1993). Gone is the notion of learning as mental reorganisation. In its place is a view of learning as intersubjective and dialogical. Learning is about participation and engagement in shared cultural practices. It involves the acquisition of 'both the organising conceptual theories and the patterns of discourse used by particular reasoning communities' (Resnick *et al.*, 1997, p.4).

Were we to follow the argument regarding the socio-construction of knowledge to its logical conclusion then we would be left with a view of cognition being not only coconstructed but also *distributed* between people. In strong form, the argument would be that knowledge inheres in relationships and only exists whilst those relationships remain intact. If these relationships become void, the conditions of distribution no longer apply, and it is not clear what, if anything, the individual is left 'knowing'. At limit, there is a 'person-in-situation, but no personal history' (Snow, 1994, p.7). As Resnick *et al.* remark: 'the situativity point of view seems to make the individual disappear or at least to exist only when particular others are about. It is as if the individual were recreated *de novo* in each new situation' (1997, p.5).

Whilst we agree with the proposition that ways of thinking are embedded in the use of language in social context and that learning is intersubjective and dialogical, we reject a 'strong' version of this approach on the grounds that it risks such ontological nihilism (Light, Sheldon and Woodhead, 1991). What is needed is an approach which respects the fundamentally social nature of cognition and yet at the same time does not unduly diminish the status of the individual. The 'problem' of situating the individual in relation to such an account of cognition is acknowledged by Resnick et al., who appeal to a notion of a 'history of experience':

. . . think of individuals as passing through a series of temporally linked situations. In each situation, the individual brings to a new interaction, with a particular set of other people and artefacts, a brain tuned to respond easily and automatically to particular affordances and constraints. When tunings and affordances are sufficiently matched, the individual can enter into the particular interactive situation, both responding to others and shaping their responses so that a mutually constituted set of cognitive actions is possible. (Resnick et al. 1997, p.5).

There is some merit in invoking the concept of a 'history of experience', but greater emphasis needs to be placed on the processes of individual construction. Contemporary situated and discursive approaches to learning take the view that the small group or dyad is 'the crucible of social meaning' while culture is 'the main resource for frameworks of meaning' (Haste, 1993, p. 186). Accepting this, it also remains the case that children are agents in their own social construction. Cole (1996) articulates this nicely in observing that mind emerges in joint activity and that there is a pivotal role for interpretation. This claim hints at the sense in which there is a dialectical relationship between the transformative changes on the intra-mental and inter-mental planes. To this extent the individual can be conceived of 'as group' and the structure of agency understood through an analysis of group functioning (Wertsch, Tulviste and Hagstrom, 1993). But this is not at all the same as saying that agency is solely an *inter*personal matter. Agency is an individual/cultural dialectic, with development and learning emerging in activities situated in particular institutional or cultural settings. Children, for example, may appropriate the particular forms of language, or 'discourses', characteristic of formal schooling. In doing so, they are also appropriating culturally constructed ways of thinking. But appropriation is an action, undertaken by an agent, and that agency is not negated by the appropriation.

The cultural context of collaboration

By invoking a notion of agency as interpersonal and socio-cultural we acknowledge the need to understand processes of joint knowledge construction, through careful analyses of discourse which focus on the continual, subtle, evolutionary process of negotiation and renegotiation of meaning. We also acknowledge the need to understand the particular historical, institutional and cultural context of collaborative learning. Discourse in any socially defined setting is nested within the wider socio-cultural context (Valsiner, 1997). As Bruner puts it, learning and thinking: 'are always situated in a cultural setting and always dependent upon the utilisation of cultural resources' (1996, p.4). Learning, in other words, is culturally based, not just culturally influenced, and the groups of children we study are not undertaking their joint work 'in a vacuum'. When focusing our research efforts on microgenetic analyses of sessions of talk and joint activity we must be careful not to neglect the other important facets of the picture. We need to recognise that understanding contexts for collaborative learning involves more than understanding how the immediate joint activity is resourced. Learners' interactions are framed by, and therefore can only ever be fully understood within, the context of particular institutional structures and settings. As Crook and Light (in press) put it, our traditions of organised education have evolved various forms of community structure, and it is important that the impact of such structures is understood. Observable interactions are likely to have unobservable determinants in the histories of individuals, groups and institutions:

The social world influences the individual not only through the agency of flesh-and-blood people who converse, communicate, model or persuade, but through the social practices and objects unseen people have built up in the world around that individual. (White, 1996, xiv)

Different institutional contexts afford different opportunities for, and constraints upon, interaction. The educational practices we see today are the result of a long period of historical development, and the activities of today's students are largely circumscribed by existing practices and established materials (Crook and Light, in press; Light and Light, 1998). The implication, then, is that collaborative interactions need to be understood within their cultural niche, with reference to the broader social and historical context within which they are positioned. As Mercer highlights:

Children's interpretations of experience, the meanings they attach to their learning – will, in part, be determined by their involvement with schools and other institutions of their society. Any educationally oriented study of learning must recognise that schools have their own body of cultural knowledge, and their own ways of communicating and legitimising knowledge. (1992, p.31)

The argument that we need to understand the wider social context of collaborative working does not only apply to those who do observational research on collaborative work within classroom settings. The need to contextualise the study of collaborative learning applies equally to the experimental tradition of research. In particular, whilst they were not an integral part of on-going classroom activity, the experimental studies of collaborative activity described in the previous chapters were undertaken in school contexts and as such we need to consider the relations between the experiments and 'indigenously organised activities' (Cole, 1996, p. 250).

The phrase 'locating the experiment' was first coined by Scribner (1975) and it is a phrase which highlights that experimental tasks are not decontextualised occurrences. It also draws attention to the fact that joint activity undertaken in experimental sessions is shaped by broader dimensions of the context. Responses to experimental tasks undertaken in educational settings are influenced by contextual systems which extend far beyond the immediate interaction between experimenter and participants. By studying interactions conducted in school settings we are studying interactions in a particular 'niche'. The children we study engage in heavily contextualised discourse. Their interactions are influenced by a complex contextual system which is inseparable from how education is defined in our culture (Mercer and Fisher, 1992). It is not the case that the pupils talk explicitly about social structures. Rather, 'institutional settings are made relevant by participants as part of their own communicative practices' (Edwards, 1997, p. 33). Context does not *determine* what is said, rather the children construct through talk the context they need to support that talk (Edwards and Furlong, 1978). Educational processes thus function as a means of acquiring and sharing cultural knowledge, knowledge which contextualises subsequent activities and problems (Mercer, 1992). Social structures are thereby constituted by 'human agency and yet at the same time are the very medium of human agency'; each is transformed by the other (Giddens, 1975, p. 121).

In highlighting the need to understand the institutional context of the activity we observe, we are also highlighting the need to push back traditional disciplinary boundaries. As Cole points out:

When we reach this level of analysis we arrive at the borders of what is ordinarily counted as psychology. As a rule, the social-institutional context of action is treated as a (largely unanalysed) dichotomised independent variable . . . or left to sociologists (1996, p. 340).

Pushing at these boundaries also necessitates methodological pluralism. There is no one 'right' way to study the institutional contexts of activity. There remains a place for experimental work such as ours which offers a very particular window through which to study context and cognition. Whilst many would undoubtedly criticise our approach on the grounds that 'real' psychological processes are only to be found in naturalistic settings, we would argue that there is no one setting in which 'true' psychological functioning and processes are revealed. Contexts for studying cognition, no matter how 'ecologically valid', are always constructed. Though we have for the most part been presenting the results of experiments, we recognise that there is value in other very different approaches such as, for example, classroom ethnography. Moreover, researchers interested in educational discourse have much to learn from studying discourse in other institutional settings (Edwards, 1997). The essential nature of collaborative classroom talk will never be understood by focusing our analytic energies *solely* on the study of classrooms. Only through linking and contrasting collaborative educational discourse with that observed in other cultural settings will we gain insight into what are the particular or defining features of such talk (Edwards, 1997).

Artefacts and affordances

So far we have talked about the important sense in which learning is constituted in institutionalised discourse. However, to focus solely on discourse processes neglects a further important sense in which cognition is constituted – namely, through our use of tools and artefacts. As Goodman (1976) maintains, tools and artefacts are 'world making'. The choice of which artefact to use affects the structure of our work activity (Scribner and Cole, 1981), thereby fundamentally transforming the cognitive and communicative requirements of our actions (Säljö, 1995, p.90). Artefacts are both ideal and material. White (1996, p. xii) describes them as 'changeling objects' that are at one and the same time *things* and 'repositories of prior human thought'.

Säljö (1995) stresses that if we are to understand cognition and practical action, we must recognise that people and artefacts operate in a system that cannot be divided. There is cofunctionality to the extent that the mediational means form part of actions in situated practices. This in turn has considerable implications for the ways in which we study learning. For example, in the case of our work, we have frequently turned to the study of children working together at a computer. The computer is an artefact which is not only capable of supporting collaborative endeavour, but has the potential to transform the way in which collaborative activity is organised. This requires us to conceptualise the role of the computer in framing and mediating joint activity.

Understanding the mediating role of the computer is a recurrent theme in much recent work. The research literature has offered a number of striking illustrations of the ways in which computer software structures and re-organises the social processes of problem solving and teaching and learning (Järvelä, 1995, Golay-Schilter, Perret, Perret-Clermont and De Guglielmo, 1998). Our own work has also highlighted the role computer equipment and interface devices play in mediating joint activity. For example, in the case of the studies described in Chapter 2, the use of a keyboard dual input device was vital in ensuring that the children engaged with one another as well as with the task in hand.

It is important to remember, however, that we never experience artefacts in isolation, but only in connection with a contextual whole. An object '. . . is always a special part, phase or aspect of an environing experienced world' (Dewey, 1938, p.67). So a child's reaction to and performance on a computer task may be crucially determined by the context of activity within which the task is encountered. The work discussed in Chapters 5 and 6, where we investigated the effects of differential contextualisation on individual girls' and boys' performance on computer-based problem-solving and perceptual-motor skills tasks, bears striking testimony to this. Even with highly constrained tasks, seemingly small changes to the contextualisation of the task can be highly significant. Moreover such changes can affect not just the absolute difficulty of a task, but also its *relative* difficulty for different groups of children.

Whilst these studies represent powerful demonstrations of the interrelationship between learner and context, the findings are often hard to interpret. Consider for example the case of the work on the perceptual-motor skills task described in Chapter 6. We rehearsed there numerous possible explanations for these findings. Our inability to settle on a preferred explanation highlights the difficulties associated with interpreting apparent 'failure' under such circumstances. We are confronted with both the necessity and the difficulty of adopting the child's point of view regarding the task in hand, and the importance of attempting to understand a participant's goals and frame of reference, as opposed to working with our own assumptions concerning what these are or should be.

As researchers, we are so often bounded by our own subjectivity and our motivating research questions that we fail to 'decentre' sufficiently to recognise or adopt other interpretative frameworks and points of view. As Grossen and Perret-Clermont's (1997) analyses of researcher–child interaction in experimental contexts illustrates, our own limited interpretations of what counts as a good, correct or appropriate response in such settings mean that we often fail to recognise the creative responses children make in such settings. All too often we treat children as objects *of concern*, rather than people *with concerns* (Prout, 1998). As psychologists we may be locked into a process of 'negative scholarly rationalism' (Säljö,

1997). We readily attribute children's behaviour to psychological incompetence, rather than seeking to develop our understanding of the activity of the child in context. Rather than theorising incompetence, we need to understand how the situations in which children are working and the meanings they ascribe to tasks support or constrain their activity and performance. Thus:

So long as psychologists continue to work within a conventional 'developmental' framework, they will be open to the charge that they emphasise relative incompetence, immaturity and dependency in ways that implicitly diminish children's status. . . . Notions of 'competence' [should be] viewed as problematic, informed by cultural beliefs and negotiated by participants in particular social contexts. (Woodhead, Faulkner and Littleton, 1999)

The implication of this line of argument is that we need to do more than simply be *open* to different interpretations of our research findings. We need to recognise that a child's performance in experimental test situations is *always* situated. It is not simply the case that some experimental tests are somehow 'fairer' than others and are therefore better at 'revealing' children's competence. Children's performance in a test situation represents the 'tuning of particular persons to the particular demands and opportunities of a situation, and thus resides in the combination of person-in-situation, not "in the mind" alone' (Snow, 1994, p. 31).

If we accept the idea of 'person-in-situation' as the appropriate unit of analysis, then the concept of 'affordance' (Gibson, 1977) is relevant. Put simply, the term 'affordance' refers to what a situation offers a person. As Snow makes clear, the term implies:

a complementarity of person and situation, as in an ecological niche . . . Affordances reflect the invitation, demand, or opportunity structure of a situation for those persons who are tuned or prepared to receive them. Particular affordances invite particular actions. The potential actions of which a person is capable are called effectivities . . . Abilities are thus unique coalitions of affordances and effectivities in particular person-treatment systems. (Snow, 1994, pp. 28–29)

The conception of abilities as linked to affordances emphasises the importance of the 'attunement' between person and situation. Moreover, if the person-in-situation becomes our analytic unit then we need to understand more about how people come to be 'tuned' and how and why they perceive particular affordances in a situation. Objects may in some sense signal their affordances, but attunement is not just about the child making sense of the world of objects. Situations are psychological spaces as well as physical spaces requiring what Rommetveit (1990) calls an attunement to the attunement of others. Children's responses and reactions to the tasks psychologists give them are crucially dependent upon the negotiation of the experimental or didactic contract (Grossen and Pochon, 1997), and the coconstruction of meaning between experimenter and child. As Grossen and Pochon note, test situations are 'communication situations that are culturally rooted and whose meanings have to be constructed intersubjectively during the interaction' (1997, p. 269).

Learning, identity and the social basis of development

Approaching the study of child development and learning in social and cultural contexts involves abandoning 'the conventional demarcation between cognitive, social and emotional development' (Woodhead, Faulkner and Littleton, 1998, p. 1). It no longer makes sense to say that we need to study the social and emotional *dimensions* of learning as if such dimensions were analytically separate and distinct from the activity of learning itself. One of the key features of a social/emotional approach to cognition is the recognition that the processes of thinking and identity construction go hand in hand:

to think or to reason well in a situation is, by definition, to take on the forms as well as the substance of a community of reasoners and thus to join that community. Much of discourse, and thus [much] of cognition serves to situate an individual with respect to others, to establish a social role or identity (Resnick, Pontecorvo and Säljö 1997, p. 9)

The importance of identity, and the ways in which children position themselves with respect to a task or their peers, was demonstrated in Chapters 5 and 6. Here we have seen how attributions and perceptions of expertise are vital elements in cognitive activity. From a very early age children are engaged in the construction of their identities as pupils. They construct and participate in discourses about ability and effort (Bird, 1994) and are motivated to understand what it means to be a learner and what it means to succeed at educational tasks. The social climate of comparison, competition, success, failure and issues of relative status in the classroom rapidly becomes established within the early years of schooling (Crocker and Cheesman, 1988) and remains a powerful interpersonal dynamic throughout children's educational careers.

This view of development and learning being sketched here has far reaching implications for the way we as developmental psychologists 'do' our science. Developmental psychology is a partial science; a science of invention, not of discovery. Simple faith in the objectivity of scientific testing will not suffice. What is needed is a detailed understanding of issues of subjectivity, intersubjectivity and social construction. We are not engaged in the activity of discovering the 'real' capabilities of the child.

Rather we are involved in the business of constructing particular accounts and representations of the child and notions of competence (Woodhead, Faulkner and Littleton, 1999). The representations we create are historically located, culturally determined and value-laden, as are the very issues we choose to investigate. As Burman puts it: 'the developmental psychology we know is tied to the culture which produced it' (Burman, 1999). Our own interest in children's use of information and communications technology, for example, has clearly been shaped by unarticulated cultural preconceptions about the contexts, goals and processes of development in Western society at the end of the twentieth century (Woodhead, Faulkner and Littleton, 1999).

Developmental psychologists do not exist in isolation from the social contexts they study. We too are 'situated' in particular institutional, cultural and historical contexts and it is in such contexts that we actively create our subject. Developmental theories and research shape the environments in which children develop and learn, and to this extent psychologists participate in the construction of contemporary reality (Rose, 1990; Woodhead, 1999). The psychologist, in this sense, is in no different a position to any other learner, engaged in a continuing intersubjective negotiation of meaning within the ever-present constraints of the material world.

Our hope is that the approach we have arrived at here will illuminate some educational as well as some psychological issues. In an era of 'standardised assessment tests' and the like, designed to drive up educational standards by highlighting individual success and failure, there may be merit in drawing attention to the social and relational bases of such achievements. We have seen that 'two heads can be better than one' and that 'wholes can be more than the sum of their parts'. We have presented evidence that the exercise as well as the acquisition of understanding is underpinned by complex social processes. Learning, whether in the classroom or in cyberspace, is a process of engagement with culturally elaborated and socially mediated reality. The social processes which shape such learning are, on the evidence we have reviewed, powerful in their effects. The harnessing of these processes to support children's learning holds the key to enhancing the effectiveness of their education, in the widest sense. If the studies gathered together in this volume contribute in some small way to this objective, then they will have served their purpose.

References

Ames, C. (1981) 'Competitive vs. cooperative reward structures: The influence of individual and group performance factors on achievement, attributions and affect', *American Educational Research Journal*, 18, pp. 273–87.

Azmitia, M. and Montgomery, R. (1993) 'Friendship, transactive dialogues, and the development of scientific reasoning', *Social Development*, 2, pp. 202–21.

Barber, M. (1994) *Young people and their attitudes to school (Interim Report)*, Keele, University Centre for Successful Schools.

Barbieri, M. S. and Light, P. (1992) 'Interaction, gender and performance on a computer based problem solving task', *Learning and Instruction*, 2, pp. 199–214.

Barron, A. and Foot, H. (1991) 'Peer tutoring and tutor training', *Educational Research*, 33, pp. 174–85.

Bennett, N., Desforges, C., Cockburn, A. and Wilkinson, B. (1984) *The Quality of Pupils' Learning Experiences*, London, Erlbaum.

Berndt, T., Perry, T. and Miller, K. (1988) 'Friends' and classmates' interactions on academic tasks', *Journal of Educational Psychology*, 80, pp. 506–13.

Beynon, J. (1993) 'Computers, dominant boys and invisible girls: Or "Hannah, it's not a toaster, it's a computer!"' in Beynon, J. and MacKay, H. (eds.) *Computers into Classrooms: More Questions than Answers*, London, Falmer Press.

Bird, L. (1994) 'Creating the capable body: Discourses about ability and effort in primary and secondary school studies' in Mayall, B. (ed.) *Children's Childhoods: Observed and Experienced*, London, Falmer Press.

Blaye, A. and Light, P. (1995) 'The influence of peer interaction on planning and information handling strategies' in O'Malley, C. (ed.) *Computer Supported Collaborative Learning*, Berlin, Springer Verlag.

Blaye, A., Light, P., Joiner, R. and Sheldon, S. (1991) 'Collaboration as a facilitator of planning and problem solving', *British Journal of Developmental Psychology*, 9, pp. 471–83.

Bliss, J., Askew, M. and Macrae, S. (1996) 'Effective teaching and learning: Scaffolding revisited', *Oxford Review of Education*, 22 (1), pp. 37–61.

Bond, C. and Titus, L. (1983) 'Social facilitation: A meta-analysis of 241 studies', *Psychological Bulletin*, 94, pp. 265–92.

Bone, A. (1983) *Girls and Girls-only Schools: A Review of the Evidence*, Manchester, Equal Opportunities Commission.

Bruner, J. (1985) 'Vygotsky: A historical and conceptual perspective' in Wertsch, J. (ed.) *Culture, Communication and Cognition: Vygotskian Perspectives*, Cambridge, Cambridge University Press.

Bruner, J. (1996) *The Culture of Education*, Cambridge, MA, Harvard University Press.

Buckley, P. and Smith, P. (1991) 'Opting out of technology: A study of girls' GCSE choices' in Lovegrove, G. and Segal, B. (eds.) *Women into Computing*, Heidelberg, Springer-Verlag.

Burman, E. (1999) 'Morality and the goals of development' in Woodhead, M., Faulkner, D. and Littleton, K. (eds.) *Making Sense of Social Development*, London, Routledge, 170–80.

Burnham, W. (1905) 'The group as a stimulus to mental activity', *Science*, 31, pp. 761–76.

Butler, R. and Ruzany, N. (1993) 'Age and socialisation effects on the development of social comparison motives and normative ability assessment in kibbutz and urban children', *Child Development*, 64, pp. 532–43.

Butterworth, G. and Light, P. (1982) *Social Cognition: Studies in the Development of Understanding*, Chicago, University of Chicago Press.

Camp, T. (1997) 'The incredible shrinking pipeline', *Communications of the Association for Computing Machinery (ACM)*, 40 (10), pp. 103–11.

Clements, D. (1987) 'A longitudinal study of the effects of Logo programming on cognitive abilities and achievement', *Journal of Educational Computing Research*, 3 (1), pp 73–94.

Clements, D. and Nastasi, B. (1992) 'The role of social interaction in the development of higher order thinking in Logo environments' in De Corte, E., Linn, M., Mandl, H. and Verschaffel, L. (eds.) *Computer-Based Learning Environments and Problem Solving*, Berlin, Springer-Verlag.

Cole, M. (1996) *Cultural Psychology: A Once and Future Discipline*, Cambridge, MA, The Belknap Press of Harvard University Press.

Cooper, J., Hall, J. and Huff, C. (1990) 'Situational stress as a consequence of sex-stereotyped software', *Personality and Social Psychology Bulletin*, 16, pp. 419–29.

Costa, E. (1991). 'The present and future of intelligent tutoring systems' in Scanlon, E. and O'Shea, T. (eds.) *New Directions in Educational Technology*, Berlin, Springer-Verlag.

Cottrell, N., Wack, D., Sekerak G. and Rittle, R. (1968) 'Social facilitation of dominant responses by the presence of an audience and the mere presence of others', *Journal of Personality and Social Psychology*, 47, pp. 1391–98.

Crocker, T. and Cheesman, R. (1988) 'The ability of young children to rank themselves for academic ability', *Educational Studies* 14 (1), pp. 105–10.

Crook, C. (1987) 'Computers in the classroom: Defining a social context' in Rutkowska, J. and Crook, C. (eds.) *Computers, Cognition and Development*, Chichester, Wiley.

Crook, C. (1994) *Computers and the Collaborative Experience of Learning*, London, Routledge.

Crook, C. and Light, P. (in press) 'Information technology and the culture of student learning' in Bliss, J., Light, P. and Säljö, R. (eds.) *Learning Sites: Social and Technological Contexts for Learning*, Oxford, Pergamon.

Culley, L. (1988) 'Girls, boys and computers', *Educational Studies*, 14, pp. 3–8.

Culley, L. (1993) 'Gender equity and computing in secondary schools' in Beynon, J. and MacKay, H. (eds.) *Computers into Classrooms: More Questions than Answers*, London, Falmer Press.

Cummings, R. (1985) 'Small group discussions and the microcomputer', *Journal of Computer Assisted Learning*, 1, pp. 149–58.

Dalton, D. (1990) 'The effects of cooperative learning strategies on achievement and attitudes', *Journal of Computer Based Instruction*, 17, pp. 8–16.

Davies, J. and Brember, I. (1995) 'Attitudes to school and the curriculum in Year 2, Year 4 and Year 6: Changes over four years', Paper presented at the European Conference on Educational Research (ECER), Bath, England, September.

De Corte, E., Verschaffel, L. and Schrooten, H. (1992) 'Cognitive effects of learning to program in Logo' in De Corte, E., Linn, M., Mandl, H. and Verschaffel, L. (eds.) *Computer-Based Learning Environments and Problem Solving*, Berlin, Springer-Verlag.

Dewey, J. (1938) *Experience and Education*, New York, Macmillan.

Doise, W. (1990) 'The development of individual competencies through social interaction' in Foot, H. Morgan, M. and Shute, R. (eds.) *Children Helping Children*, Chichester, John Wiley.

Doise, W. and Mugny, G. (1984) *The Social Development of the Intellect*, Oxford, Pergamon.

Doise, W., Mugny, G. and Perret-Clermont, A.-N. (1975) 'Social interaction and the development of cognitive operations', *European Journal of Social Psychology*, 5, pp. 367–83.

Doise, W., Mugny, G. and Perret-Clermont, A.-N. (1976) 'Social interaction and cognitive development', *European Journal of Social Psychology*, 6, pp. 245–47.

Donaldson, M. (1978) *Children's Minds*, London, Fontana.

Durkin, K. (1995) *Developmental Social Psychology*, Oxford, Blackwell.

Edwards, D. (1997) 'Towards a discursive psychology of classroom education' in Coll, C. and Edwards, D. (eds.) *Teaching, Learning and Classroom Discourse*, Madrid, Fundación Infancia y Aprendizaje.

Edwards, D. and Furlong, V. (1978) *The Language of Teaching and Learning*, London, Heinemann.

Edwards, D. and Mercer, N. (1987) *Common Knowledge: The Development of Understanding in the Classroom*, London, Methuen.

Festinger, L. (1954) 'A theory of social comparison processes', *Human Relations*, 7, pp. 117–40.

Fitzpatrick, H. (1996) 'Peer collaboration and the computer', Unpublished PhD thesis, University of Manchester.

Fitzpatrick, H. and Hardman, M. (1994) 'Gender and the classroom computer: Do girls lose out?' in Foot, H., Howe, C., Anderson, A., Tolmie, A. and Warden, D. (eds.) *Group and Interactive Learning*, Southampton, Computational Mechanics Publications.

Flynn, E. (1995) 'The effects of own gender and partner gender on children's computer-based problem solving in the context of a single sex school', Unpublished dissertation, Department of Psychology, University of Southampton.

Forman, E. and Cazden, C. (1985) 'Exploring Vygotskian perspectives in education: The cognitive value of peer interaction' in Wertsch, J. (ed.) *Culture, Communication and Cognition: Vygotskian Perspectives*, Cambridge, Cambridge University Press.

Forman, E., Minick, N. and Stone, A. (1993) *Contexts for Learning: Sociocultural Dynamics in Children's Development*, Oxford, Oxford University Press.

Gabrenya, W., Wang, Y. and Latane, B. (1985) 'Social loafing on an optimising task: Cross cultural differences amongst Chinese and Americans', *Journal of Cross Cultural Psychology*, 16, pp. 223–42.

Galton, M. and Williamson, J. (1992) *Groupwork in the Primary School*, London, Routledge.

Gardner, J., McEwan, A. and Curry, C. (1985) 'A sample survey of attitudes to computer studies', *Computers and Education*, 10, pp. 293–98.

Gauvain, M. and Rogoff, B. (1989) 'Collaborative problem solving and children's planning skills', *Developmental Psychology*, 25, pp. 131–51.

Gergen, K. (1977) 'The social comparison of self knowledge' in Mischel, T. (ed.) *The Self: Psychological and Biological Issues*, NJ, Rowman and Littlefield.

Giacquinta, J., Bauer, J. and Levin, J. (1993) *Beyond Technology's Promise*, Cambridge, Cambridge University Press.

Gibson, J. (1977) 'The theory of affordances' in Shaw, R. and Bransford, J. (eds.) *Perceiving, Acting and Knowing: Toward an Ecological Psychology*, Hillsdale, NJ, Lawrence Erlbaum.

Giddens, A. (1975) *New Rules of Sociological Method*, New York, Basic Books.

Glachan, M. and Light, P. (1982) 'Peer interaction and learning: Can two wrongs make a right?' in Butterworth, G. and Light, P. (eds.) *Social Cognition: Studies of the Development of Understanding*, Brighton, Harvester Press.

Glaser, A. (1982) 'Drive theory of social facilitation: A critical appraisal', *British Journal of Social Psychology*, 21, pp. 265–82.

Golay-Schilter, D., Perret, J.-F., Perret-Clermont, A.-N. and De Guglielmo, F. (1999) 'Socio-cognitive interactions in a computerised industrial task: Are they productive for learning?' in Littleton, K. and Light, P. (eds.) *Learning with Computers: Analysing Productive Interaction*, London, Routledge.

Goodman, N. (1976) *Languages of Art*, Indianapolis, IN, Hackett.

Graddol, D. and Swann, J. (1989) *Gender Voices*, Oxford, Blackwell.

Greenfield, T. (1995) 'Sex differences in science museum exhibit attraction', *Journal of Research in Science Teaching*, 32, pp. 925–38.

Greenfield, P., Brannon, C. and Lohr, D. (1994). 'Two dimensional representation of movement through three dimensional space: The role of video-game experience', *Journal of Applied Developmental Psychology*, 15, pp. 87–103.

Greenfield, P. and Lave, J. (1982) 'Cognitive aspects of informal education' in Wagner, D. and Stephenson, H. (eds.) *Cultural Perspectives on Child Development*, San Francisco, Freeman.

Griffiths, M. (1991) 'Amusement machine playing in childhood and adolescence: A comparative analysis of video games and fruit machines', *Journal of Adolescence*, 14 , pp. 53–73.

Griffiths, M. (1996) 'Computer game playing in children and adolescents: A review of the literature' in Gill, T. (ed.) *Electronic Children: How Children are Responding to the Information Revolution*, London, National Children's Bureau.

Grossen, M. (1988) 'La construction sociale de l'intersubjectivité entre adult et enfant en situation de test', PhD thesis, University of Neuchatel, Switzerland.

Grossen, M. and Perret-Clermont, A.-N. (1997) 'Learning: A reproduction of institutionalised teaching practices or a personal appropriation', Paper presented at the Seventh European Conference for Research on Learning and Instruction, Athens, August.

Grossen, M. and Pochon, L.-C. (1997) 'Interactional perspectives on the use of the computer and on the technological development of a new tool: The case of word processing' in Resnick, L., Säljö, R., Pontecorvo, C. and Burge, B. (eds.) *Discourse, Tools and Reasoning: Essays on Situated Cognition*, Berlin and New York, SpringerVerlag.

Hartley, J. (1968) 'Some factors affecting student performance in programmed learning', *Programmed Learning and Educational Technology*, 5, pp. 206–18.

Hartley, J. and Hogarth, F. (1971) 'Programmed learning in pairs', *Educational Research*, 13, pp. 130–34.

Hartwick, J. and Nagao, D. (1990) 'Social facilitation effects in recognition memory', *British Journal of Social Psychology*, 29, pp. 193–210.

Haste, H. (1993) 'Morality, self and sociohistorical context: The role of lay social theory' in Noam, G. and Wren, T. (eds.) *The Moral Self*, Cambridge, MA, MIT Press.

Hattie, J. and Fitzgerald. D. (1988) 'Sex differences in attitudes, achievement and use of computers', *Australian Journal of Education*, 31, pp. 3–26.

Healy, L., Pozzi, S. and Hoyles, C. (1995) 'Making sense of groups, computers and mathematics', *Cognition and Instruction*, 13, pp. 505–23.

Hogan, D. and Tudge, J. (in press) 'Implications of Vygotskian theory for learning' in O'Donnel, A. and King, A. (eds.) *Cognitive Perspectives on Peer Learning*, Matwah, NJ, Lawrence Erlbaum Associates.

Howe, C. and Tolmie, A. (1999) 'Productive interaction in the context of computer supported collaborative learning in science' in Littleton, K. and Light, P. (eds.) *Learning with Computers: Analysing Productive Interaction*, London, Routledge.

Howe, C., Tolmie, A., Anderson, A. and Mackenzie, M. (1992) 'Conceptual knowledge in physics: The role of group interaction in computer supported teaching', *Learning and Instruction*, 2, pp. 161–84.

Hoyles, C. (ed.) (1988) *Girls and Computers*, London, Institute of Education, Bedford Way Papers, 34.

Hoyles, C. and Sutherland, R. (1989) *Logo Mathematics in the Classroom*, London, Routledge.

Hoyles, C., Sutherland, R. and Healy, L. (1991) 'Children talking in computer environments' in Durkin, K. and Shire, B. (eds.) *Language in Mathematical Education: Research and Practice*, Milton Keynes, Open University Press.

Hughes, M. (1990) 'Children's computation' in Grieve, R. and Hughes, M. (eds.) *Understanding Children*, Oxford, Blackwell.

Hughes, M., Brackenridge, A., Bibby, A. and Greenhough, P. (1988) 'Girls, boys and turtles: Gender effects in young children's learning with Logo' in Hoyles, C. (ed.) *Girls and Computers*, London, Institute of Education, Bedford Way Papers, 34.

Hughes, M., Brackenridge, A. and MacLeod, H. (1987) 'Children's ideas about computers' in Rutkowska, J. and Crook, C. (eds.) *Computers, Cognition and Development*, Chichester: John Wiley.

Hughes, M., Greenhough, P. and Laing, K. (1992) 'Gender effects in young children learning Logo'. Final report to the Nuffield Foundation, Exeter: School of Education, University of Exeter.

Huguet, P., Charbonnier, E. and Monteil, J.-M. (1995) 'Where does self-esteem come from? The influence of private vs. public individuation', *Social Behavior and Personality*, 23, pp. 70–81.

Humphreys, J. (1995) 'Gender effects on children's performance on the Tower of Hanoi as a manual and a computer task', Unpublished dissertation, Department of Psychology, University of Southampton.

Hutchins, G., Hall, W. and Colbourn, C. (1993) 'Patterns of students' interactions with hypermedia systems', *Interacting with Computers*, 5, pp. 295–313.

Inhelder, B. and Piaget, J. (1958) *The Growth of Logical Thinking from Childhood to Adolescence*. New York: Basic Books.

Jackson, A., Fletcher, B. and Messer, D. (1986) 'A survey of microcomputer use and provision in primary schools', *Journal of Computer Assisted Learning*, 2, pp. 45–55.

Janssen Reinen, I. and Plomp, T. (1997) 'Information technology and gender equality: A contradiction in terms?', *Computers and Education*, 28 (2), pp. 65–78.

Järvelä, S. (1995) 'The cognitive apprenticeship model in a technologically rich learning environment: Interpreting the learning interaction', *Learning and Instruction*, 5 (3), pp. 237–59.

Johnson, D. and Johnson, R. (1986) 'Computer assisted cooperative learning', *Educational Technology*, January, 12–18.

Joiner, R., Messer, D., Light, P. and Littleton, K. (1994) 'Talking and learning: A preliminary investigation into productive interaction' in

Foot, H., Howe, C., Anderson, A. Tolmie, A. and Warden, D. (eds.) *Group and Interactive Learning*, Southampton, Computational Mechanics Publications.

Joiner, R., Messer, D., Steele, F., Light, P. and Littleton, K. (1993) 'Peer presence, gender and computer experience in computer based problem solving', Paper presented at the ESRC InTER Seminar on Collaborative Learning, Oxford, February.

Karau, S. and Williams, K. (1993) 'Social loafing: A meta-analytic review and theoretical integration', *Journal of Personality and Social Psychology*, 29, pp. 135–74.

Kirkup, G. (1992) 'The social construction of computers' in Kirkup, G. and Keller, S. (eds.) *Inventing Women: Science, Gender and Technology*, Oxford, Polity Press.

Kliman, M. (1985) 'A new approach to infant and early primary Mathematics', DAI Research Paper 241, Edinburgh: Department of Artificial Intelligence, University of Edinburgh.

Kluger, A. and DeNisi, A. (1996) 'The effects of feedback interventions on performance: A historical review, a meta-analysis and a preliminary feedback intervention theory', *Psychological Bulletin*, 119, pp. 254–84.

Kutnick, P. and Rogers, C. (eds.) (1994) *Groups in Schools*, London, Cassell.

Lave, J. and Wenger, E. (1991) *Situated Learning: Legitimate Peripheral Participation*, Cambridge, Cambridge University Press.

Lee, M. (1993) 'Gender, group composition and peer interaction in computer based co-operative learning', *Journal of Educational Computing Research*, 4, pp. 549–77.

Light, P. (1979) *The Development of Social Sensitivity*, Cambridge, Cambridge University Press.

Light, P. (1986) 'Context, conservation and conversation' in Richards, M. and Light, P. (eds.) *Children of Social Worlds*, Cambridge, Polity Press.

Light, P. (1994) 'Peer interaction and peer comparison as facilitators of children's learning', Invited Plenary Address, First International Conference on Group and Interactive Learning, Glasgow, September.

Light, P. (1997) 'Computers for learning: Psychological perspectives', *Journal of Child Psychology and Psychiatry*, 38 (5), pp. 497–504.

Light, P., Buckingham, N. and Robbins, A. (1979) 'The conservation task as an interactional setting', *British Journal of Educational Psychology*, 49, pp. 304–10.

Light, P. and Colbourn, C. (1987) 'The role of social processes in children's microcomputer use' in Kent, W. and Lewis, R. (eds.) *Computer Assisted Learning in the Social Sciences and Humanities*, Oxford, Blackwell.

Light, P. and Foot, T. (1987) 'Peer interaction and microcomputer use' *Rassegna di Psicologia*, 4, pp. 93–104.

Light, P., Foot, T., Colbourn, C. and McClelland, I. (1987) 'Collaborative interactions at the microcomputer keyboard', *Educational Psychology*, 7, pp. 13–21.

Light, P. and Gilmour, A. (1983) 'Conservation or conversation? Contextual facilitation of inappropriate conservation judgements', *Journal of Experi-*

mental Child Psychology, 36, pp. 356–63.

Light, P. and Glachan, M. (1985) 'Peer interaction and problem solving', *Educational Psychology*, 5, pp. 217–25.

Light, P., Gorsuch, C. and Newman, J. (1987) 'Why do you ask? Context and communication in the conservation task', *European Journal of Psychology of Education*, 2, pp. 73–82.

Light, P. and Light, V. (1999) 'Reaching for the sky: Computer supported tutorial interaction in a conventional university setting' in Littleton, K. and Light, P. (eds.) *Learning with Computers: Analysing productive interaction*, London, Routledge.

Light, P., Littleton, K., Bale, S., Messer, D. and Joiner, R. (in press) 'Gender and social comparison effects in computer based problem solving', *Learning and Instruction*.

Light, P., Littleton, K., Messer, D. and Joiner, R. (1994) 'Social and communicative processes in computer based learning', *European Journal of Psychology of Education*, 9, pp. 93–109.

Light, P. and Nix, C. (1983) '"Own view" versus "good view" in a perspective-taking task' *Child Development*, 54, pp. 480–83.

Light, P. and Perret-Clermont, A-N. (1991) 'Social context effects in learning and testing' in Light, P., Sheldon, S. and Woodhead, M. (eds.) *Learning to Think*, London, Routledge.

Light, P., Sheldon, S. and Woodhead, M. (eds.) (1991) *Learning to Think*, London, Routledge.

Linnakylä, P. (1996) 'High expectations – High achievement on literacy', Paper presented at the 1996 World Conference on Literacy, Philadelphia, March 12–15.

Littleton, K. (1995) 'Children and Computers' in Bancroft, D. and Carr, R. (eds.) *Influencing Children's Development*, Oxford, Blackwell.

Littleton, K. (1996) 'Girls and information technology' in Murphy, P. and Gipps, C. (eds.) *Equity in the classroom: Towards an Effective Pedagogy for Girls and Boys*, London, Falmer Press/UNESCO Publishing.

Littleton, K., Ashman, H., Light, P., Artis, J., Roberts, T. and Oosterwegel, A. (1999) 'Gender, task contexts and children's performance on a computer-based task', *European Journal of Psychology of Education*.

Littleton, K. and Bannert, M. (in press) 'Gender and IT: Contextualising difference' in Bliss, J., Light, P. and Säljö, R. (eds.) *Learning Sites: Social and Technological Contexts for Learning*, Oxford: Pergamon.

Littleton, K., Light, P., Joiner, R., Messer, D. and Barnes, P. (1992) 'Pairing and gender effects on children's computer-based learning', *European Journal of Psychology of Education*, 7, pp. 311–24.

Littleton, K., Light, P., Joiner, R., Messer, D. and Barnes, P. (1998) 'Gender, task scenarios and children's computer-based problem solving', *Educational Psychology*, 18 (3), pp. 327–40.

Littleton, K., Light, P., Robertson, A. and Beeton, A. (in preparation) 'A task by any other name . . . ? Academic attainment, task contexts, and children's on-task performance'.

Lockheed, M., Nielson, A. and Stone, M. (1985) 'Determinants of microcomputer literacy in high school students', *Journal of Educational Computing Research*, 1, pp. 81–96.

McGarrigle, J. and Donaldson, M. (1975) 'Conservation accidents', *Cognition*, 3, pp. 341–50.

Manstead, A. and Semin, G. (1980) 'Social facilitation effects: Mere enhancement of dominant response?', *British Journal of Social and Clinical Psychology*, 19, pp. 119–36.

Marshall, H. and Weinstein, R. (1984) 'Classroom factors affecting students' self evaluations: An interactional model', *Review of Educational Research*, 54, pp. 301–25.

Martin, R. (1991) 'School children's attitudes towards computers as a function of gender, course subjects and availability of home computers', *Journal of Computer Assisted Learning*, 7, pp. 187–94.

Mash, E. and Hedley, J. (1975) 'Effect of observer as a function of prior history of social interaction', *Perceptual and Motor Skills*, 40, pp. 659–69.

Malone, T. (1981) 'Toward a theory of intrinsically motivating instruction', *Cognitive Science*, 4, pp. 333–69.

Mercer, N. (1992) 'Culture, context and the construction of knowledge in the classroom' in Light, P. and Butterworth, G. (eds.) *Context and Cognition: Ways of Learning and Knowing*, Hemel Hempstead, Herts, Harvester Wheatsheaf.

Mercer, N. (1995) *The Guided Construction of Knowledge*, Clevedon, Avon, Multilingual Matters.

Mercer, N. and Fisher, E. (1992) 'How do teachers help children to learn? An analysis of teachers' interventions in computer-based activities', *Learning and Instruction* , 2, pp. 339–55.

Mercer, N. and Wegerif, R. (1999) 'Is exploratory talk productive talk?' in Littleton, K. and Light, P. *Learning with Computers: Analysing Productive Interaction*, London, Routledge.

Mevarech, Z., Silber, O. and Fine, D. (1991) 'Learning with computers in small groups', *Journal of Educational Computing Research*, 7, pp. 233–43.

Miller, S. (1982) 'On the generalisability of conservation', *British Journal of Psychology*, 73, pp. 221–30.

Miller, S. and Brownell, C. (1975) 'Peers, persuasion and Piaget', *Child Development*, 46, pp. 992–97.

Monteil, J.-M. (1988) 'Comparaison sociale: Strategies individuelle et mediations socio-cognitives', *European Journal of Psychology of Education*, 3, pp. 3–18.

Monteil, J.-M. and Huguet, P. (1991) 'Insertion sociale, categorisation sociale et activites cognitives', *Psychologie Francaise*, 36, pp. 35–46.

Monteil, J.-M. and Huguet, P. (in press) *The Social Psychology of Cognition*, Hove, Erlbaum.

Mugny, G. and Doise, W. (1978) 'Socio-cognitive conflict and structures of individual and collective performances', *European Journal of Social Psychology*, 8, pp. 181–92.

Mugny, G., Perret-Clermont and Doise, A.-N. (1981) 'Interpersonal coordinations and sociological differences in the construction of the intellect' in Stevenson, G. and Davis, G. (eds.) *Applied Social Psychology*, vol. I, Chichester, Wiley.

Murphy, P. (1993) 'Assessment and gender' in Bourne, J. (ed.) *Thinking Through Primary Practice*, London, Routledge.

Murray, J. (1974) 'Social learning and cognitive development', *British Journal of Psychology*, 65, pp. 151–60.

Nathan, M. and Resnick, L. (1994) 'Less can be more: Unintelligent tutoring based on psychological theories and experimentation' in Vosniadou, S., De Corte E. and Mandl, H. (eds.) *Technology Based Learning Environments*, Berlin, Springer-Verlag.

Newman, D., Griffin, P. and Cole, M. (1989) *The Construction Zone: Working for Cognitive Change in Schools*, Cambridge, Cambridge University Press.

Newton P. and Beck E. (1993) 'Computing: An ideal occupation for women?' in Beynon, J. and MacKay, H. (eds.) *Computers into Classrooms: More Questions than Answers*, London, Falmer Press.

Niemiec, R. and Walberg, H. (1987) 'Comparative effects of computer assisted instruction: A synthesis of reviews', *Journal of Educational Computing Research*, 3, pp. 19–37.

Packer, M. (1993) 'Away from internalization' in Forman, E., Minick, N. and Stone, A. (1993) *Contexts for Learning: Sociocultural Dynamics in Children's Development*, Oxford, Oxford University Press.

Papert, S. (1980) *Mindstorms: Children, Computers and Powerful Ideas*, New York, Harvester Wheatsheaf.

Papert, S. (1994) *The Children's Machine*, London, Harvester Wheatsheaf.

Pea, R. and Kurland, M. (1984) 'The cognitive effects of learning computer programming', *New Ideas in Psychology*, 2, pp. 137–68.

Pelgrum W. and Plomp, T. (1993) *The IEA Study of Computers in Education*, Oxford, Pergamon.

Perret-Clermont, A.-N. (1980) *Social Interaction and Cognitive Development in Children*, London, Academic Press.

Pheasey, K. and Underwood, G. (1994) 'Collaboration and discourse during computer based problem solving' in Foot, H., Howe, C., Anderson, A., Tolmie, A. and Warden, D. (eds.) *Group and Interactive Learning*, Southampton, Computational Mechanics Publications.

Phelps, E. and Damon, W. (1989) 'Problem solving with equals: Peer collaboration as a context for learning mathematical and spatial concepts', *Journal of Educational Psychology*, 81, pp. 639–46.

Piaget, J. (1932) *The Moral Judgement of the Child*, London, Routledge.

Piaget, J. and Inhelder, B. (1956) *The Child's Conception of Space*, London, Routledge.

Pozzi, S., Healy, L. and Hoyles, C. (1993) 'Learning and interaction in groups with computers: When do ability and gender matter?', *Social Development*, 2, pp. 222–41.

Prout, A. (1998) *Concluding remarks*, Conference on Children and Social Exclusion, Centre for the Social Study of Childhood, Hull University.

Provenzo, E. (1991) *Video Kids: Making Sense of Nintendo*, Cambridge, MA: Harvard University Press.

Radziszewska, B. and Rogoff, B. (1988) 'Influence of adult and peer collaboration on children's planning skills', *Developmental Psychology*, 24, pp. 840–48.

Resnick, L., Pontecorvo, C. and Säljö, R. (1997) 'Discourse, tools and reasoning' in Resnick, L., Säljö, R., Pontecorvo, C. and Burge, B. (eds.) *Discourse, Tools and Reasoning: Essays on Situated Cognition*, Berlin and New York, Springer-Verlag.

Ringelmann, M. (1913) 'Recherches sur les moteurs animes: Travail de l'homme', *Annales de l'Institut Nationale Agronomique*, 12, pp. 1–40.

Roazzi, A. and Bryant, P. (1992) 'Social class, context and cognitive development' in Light, P. and Butterworth, G. (eds.) *Context and Cognition: Ways of Learning and Knowing*, Hemel Hempstead, Harvester Wheatsheaf.

Robertson, S. I., Calder, J., Fung, P., Jones, A. and O'Shea, T. (1995) 'Computer attitudes in an English secondary school', *Computers and Education*, 24, pp. 3–81.

Robinson-Staveley, K. and Cooper, J. (1990) 'Mere presence, gender and reaction to computers: Studying human–computer interaction in the social context', *Journal of Experimental Social Psychology*, 26, pp. 168–83.

Rogoff. B. (1990) *Apprenticeship in Thinking: Cognitive Development in Social Context*, Oxford, Oxford University Press.

Rogoff, B. and Gardner, W.P. (1984) 'Guidance in cognitive development: An examination of mother–child instruction', in Rogoff, B and Lave, J. (eds.) *Everyday Cognition: Its Development in Social Context*, Cambridge, MA, Harvard University Press.

Rommetveit, R. (1992) 'Outlines of a dialogically based social-cognitive approach to human cognition and communication' in Wold, A. (ed.) *The Dialogical Alternative: Towards a Theory of Language and Mind*, Oslo, Scandinavian Press.

Roschelle, J. and Teasley, S. (1995) 'The construction of shared knowledge in collaborative problem solving' in O'Malley, C. (ed.) *Computer Supported Collaborative Learning*, Berlin, Springer Verlag.

Rose, N. (1990) 'Psychology as a "social" science' in Parker, I. and Shotter, J. (eds.) *Deconstructing Social Psychology*, London, Routledge.

Rosenthal, T. and Zimmerman, B. (1972) 'Modelling by exemplification and instruction in training conservation', *Developmental Psychology*, 6, pp. 392–401.

Ruble, D. (1983) 'The development of social comparison processes and their role in achievement-related self-socialisation' in Higgins, E., Ruble, D. and Hartup, W. (eds.) *Social Cognition and Social Development: A Socio-Cultural Perspective*, Cambridge, Cambridge University Press.

Ruble, D. and Flett, G. (1988) 'Conflicting goals in self-evaluative information seeking: Developmental and ability level analyses', *Child Development*, 59, pp. 97–106.

Ruble, D. and Frey, K. (1991) 'Changing patterns of comparative behaviour as skills are acquired: A functional model of self-evaluation' in Suls, J.

and Wills, T. (eds.) *Social Comparison: Contemporary Theory and Research*, Hillsdale, NJ., Erlbaum.

Russell, J. (1981) 'Why socio-cognitive conflict may be impossible', *Educational Psychology*, 1, pp. 159–69.

Russell, J. (1982) 'Propositional attitudes' in Beveridge, M. (ed.) *Children Thinking Through Language*, London, Edward Arnold.

Säljö, R. (1995) 'Mental and physical artefacts in cognitive practices' in Reimann, P. and Spada, H. (eds.) *Learning in Humans and Machines: Towards an Interdisciplinary Learning Science*, Oxford, Pergamon.

Säljö, R. (1997) 'Heavenly talk. Discourse, artifacts and children's understanding of elementary astronomy', Seminar presentation. Milton Keynes, Open University, November.

Sanna, L. (1992) 'Self efficacy theory: Implications for social facilitation and social loafing', *Journal of Personality and Social Psychology*, 62, pp. 774–86.

Scanlon, E., Issroff, K. and Murphy, P. (1999) 'Collaborations in a primary classroom' in Littleton, K. and Light, P. (eds.) *Learning with Computers: Analysing Productive Interaction*, London, Routledge.

Schank, R. and Cleary, C. (1995) *Engines for Education*, Hillsdale, NJ, Erlbaum.

Schofield, J. (1995) *Computers and Classroom Culture*, Cambridge, Cambridge University Press.

Scribner, S. (1975) 'Situating the experiment in cross cultural research' in Riegel, K.F. and Meacham J. A. (eds.) *The Developing Individual in a Changing World: Historical and Cultural Issues*, The Hague, Mouton.

Scribner, S. and Cole, M. (1981) *The Psychology of Literacy*, Cambridge, MA, Harvard University Press.

Seta, J. and Hassan, R. (1980) 'Awareness of prior success and failure: A critical factor in task performance', *Journal of Personality and Social Psychology*, 39, pp. 70–76.

Shashaani, L. (1993) 'Gender based difference in attitudes towards computers', *Computers and Education*, 20 (2), pp. 169–81.

Sheingold, K., Hawkins, J. and Char, C. (1984) '"I'm the thinkist, you're the typist": The interaction of technology and the social life of classrooms', Technical Report 27, Bank Street College of Education, New York.

Shrock, S. and Stepp, S. (1991) 'The role of the child micro-computer expert in an elementary classroom: A theme emerging from a naturalistic study', *Journal of Research on Computing in Education*, 23 (4), pp. 545–59.

Siann, G., Durndell, A., McLeod, H. and Glissov, P. (1988) 'Stereotyping in relation to gender gap in participation in computing', *Educational Research*, 30, pp. 98–103.

Siegler, R. (1976) 'Three aspects of cognitive development', *Cognitive Psychology*, 8, pp. 481–520.

Silverman, I. and Geiringer, E. (1973) 'Dyadic interaction and conservation induction', *Child Development*, 44, pp. 815–20.

Skinner, B. F. (1965) 'Reflections on a decade of teaching machines' in

Glaser, R. (ed.) *Teaching Machines and Programmed Learning*, Washington, National Education Association.

Smith, R. (1991) 'A prototype futuristic technology for distance education' in Scanlon, E. and O'Shea, T. (eds.) *New Directions in Educational Technology*, Berlin, Springer-Verlag.

Snow, R. (1994) 'Abilities in academic tasks' in Sternberg, R. and Wagner, R. (eds.) *Mind in Context: Interactionist Perspectives on Human Intelligence*, Cambridge, Cambridge University Press.

Straker, A. (1989) *Children Using Computers*, Oxford, Blackwell.

Stutz, E. (1996) 'Is electronic entertainment hindering children's play and social development?' in Gill, T. (ed.) *Electronic Children: How Children are Responding to the Information Revolution*, London, National Children's Bureau.

Subrahmanyam, K. and Greenfield, P. (1994) 'Effect of video-game practice on spatial skills in girls and boys', *Journal of Applied Developmental Psychology*, 15, pp. 13–32.

Suchman, L. (1987) *Plans and Situated Actions*, Cambridge, Cambridge University Press.

Suppes, P. (1966) 'The use of computers in education', *Scientific American*, 215, pp. 207–20.

Swann, J. (1997) 'Tinkertown: Reading and re-reading children's talk around the computer' in Wegerif, R. and Scrimshaw, P. (eds.) *Computers and Talk in the Primary Classroom*, Clevedon, Avon, Multilingual Matters.

Tharp, R. and Gallimore, R. (1988) *Rousing Minds to Life: Teaching, Learning and Schooling in Social Context*, Cambridge, Cambridge University Press.

Tizard, B., Blatchford, P., Burke, J., Farquhar, C. and Plewis, I. (1988) *Young Children at School in the Inner City*, Hove, Erlbaum.

Todman, J. and Dick, G. (1993) 'Primary children and teachers' attitudes to computers', *Computers in Education*, 20, pp. 199–203.

Todman, J. and File, P. (1990) 'A scale for children's attitudes to computers', *School Psychology International*, 11, 71–75.

Tomasello, M., Kruger, A. and Ratner, H. (1993) 'Cultural learning', *Behavioral and Brain Sciences*, 16, pp. 495–552.

Topping, K. (1994) 'Peer tutoring' in Kutnick, P. and Rogers, C. (eds.) *Groups in Schools*, London, Cassell.

Triplett, N. (1898) 'The dynamogenic factors in pacemaking and competition' *American Journal of Psychology*, 9, pp. 507–33.

Turkle, S. and Papert, S. (1990) 'Epistemological pluralism: Styles and voices within the computer culture', *Signs: Journal of Women in Culture and Society*, 16, pp. 128–57.

Underwood, G., Jindal, N. and Underwood, J. (1994) 'Gender differences and effects of cooperation in a computer based language task', *Educational Research*, 36, pp. 63–74.

Underwood, G., McCaffrey, M. and Underwood, J. (1990) 'Gender differences in a computer based language task' *Educational Research*, 32, pp. 44–9.

Underwood, J. and Underwood, G. (1999) 'Task effects on co-operative and collaborative learning with computers' in Littleton, K. and Light, P.

(eds.) *Learning with Computers: Analysing Productive Interaction*, London, Routledge.

Valsiner, J. (1997) 'Bounded indeterminacy in discourse processes' in Coll, C. and Edwards, D. (eds.) *Teaching, Learning and Classroom Discourse*, Madrid, Fundación Infancia y Aprendizaje.

Vygotsky, L.S. (1978) *Mind in Society: The Development of Higher Psychological Processes*, Cambridge, MA, Harvard University Press.

Vygotsky, L.S. (1990) 'Genesis of the higher mental functions' in Light, P., Sheldon, S. and Woodhead, M. (eds.) *Learning to Think*, London, Routledge.

Watson, M. (1997) 'Improving group work at the computer' in Wegerif, R. and Scrimshaw, P. (eds.) *Computers and Talk in the Primary Classroom*, Clevedon, Avon, Multilingual Matters.

Webb, N., Ender, P. and Lewis, S. (1986) 'Problem solving strategies and group processes in small groups learning computer programming', *American Educational Research Journal*, 23, pp. 243–61.

Wegerif, R. and Mercer, N. (1997) 'A dialogical framework for researching peer talk' in Wegerif, R. and Scrimshaw, P. (eds.) *Computers and Talk in the Primary Classroom*, Clevedon, Avon, Multilingual Matters.

Wertsch, J. (1985) *Vygotsky and the Social Formation of Mind*, Cambridge, MA, Harvard University Press.

Wertsch, J. (1997) 'The socio-cultural approach to learning', Paper presented to an Inaugural Conference of the Centre for Learning in Organisations, School of Education, University of Bristol, January.

Wertsch, J. (1998) *Mind as Action*, Oxford, Oxford University Press.

Wertsch, J., Tulviste, P. and Hagstrom, F. (1993) 'A socio-cultural approach to agency' in Forman, E., Minick, N.and Stone, A. (1993) *Contexts for learning: Sociocultural Dynamics in Children's Development*, Oxford, Oxford University Press.

White, S. (1996) 'Foreword' in Cole, M. *Cultural Psychology: A Once and Future Discipline*, Cambridge, MA, The Belknap Press of Harvard University Press.

Whitelock, D., O'Shea, T., Taylor, J., Scanlon, E., Clark P. and O'Malley, C. (1993) 'The influence of peer interaction and peer presence in computer supported learning', Paper presented to CAL 93 Conference 'CAL into the Mainstream', York, April.

Whitley, B. (1997) 'Gender differences in computer-related attitudes and behaviour: A meta-analysis', *Computers in Human Behaviour*, 13 (1), pp. 1–22.

Wilder, G., Mackie, D. and Cooper, J. (1985) 'Gender and computers: Two surveys of computer related attitudes', *Sex Roles*, 13, pp. 215–28.

Williams, J., Harkins, S. and Latane, B. (1981) 'Identifiability as a deterrent to social loafing', *Journal of Personality and Social Psychology*, 40, pp. 303–11.

Wood, D. (1986) 'Aspects of teaching and learning'. In Richards, M and Light, P. (eds.) *Children of Social Worlds*, Cambridge, Polity Press.

Wood, D., Bruner, J. and Ross, G. (1976) 'The role of tutoring in problem solving', *Journal of Child Psychology and Psychiatry*, 17, pp. 89–100.

Wood, D. and Wood, H. (1996) 'Vygotsky, tutoring and learning', *Oxford Review of Education*, 22, pp. 5–16.

Wood, D. and Wood, H. (in press) 'Contingency in tutoring and learning', *Learning and Instruction*.

Woodhead, M. (1999) 'Reconstructing developmental psychology – Some first steps', *Children and Society*, 13 (1), 1–17.

Woodhead, M, Faulkner, D. and Littleton, K. (eds.) (1998) *Cultural Worlds of Early Childhood*, London, Routledge.

Woodhead, M. Faulkner, D. and Littleton, K. (eds.) (1999) *Making Sense of Social Development*, London, Routledge.

Zajonc, R. (1965) 'Social facilitation', *Science*, 149, pp. 269–74.

Index

Compiled by Judith Lavender

Imitation in Infancy

Jacqueline Nadel and George Butterworth

This is the first book to bring together the extensive modern evidence for innate imitation in babies. Modern research has shown imitation to be a natural mechanism of learning and communication which deserves to be at centre stage in developmental psychology. Yet the very possibility of imitation in newborn humans has had a controversial history. Defining imitation has proved to be far from straightforward and scientific evidence for its existence in neonates is only now becoming accepted, despite more than a century of enquiry. In this book, some of the world's foremost researchers on imitation and intellectual development review evidence for imitation in newborn babies. They discuss the development of imitation in infancy, in both normal and atypical populations and in comparison with other primate species, stressing the fundamental importance of imitation in human development, as a foundation of communication and a precursor to symbolic processes.

Learning to Read and Write: A Cross-Linguistic Perspective

Margaret Harris and Giyoo Hatano

For many years, the development of theories about the way children learn to read and write was dominated by studies of English-speaking populations. As we have learned more about the way that children learn to read and write other scripts – whether they have less regularity in their grapheme–phoneme correspondences or do not make use of alphabetic symbols in all – it has become clear that many of the difficulties that confront children learning to read and write English specifically are less evident, or even non-existent, in other populations. At the same time, some aspects of learning to read and write are very similar across scripts. The unique cross-linguistic perspective offered in this book, including chapters on Japanese, Greek and the Scandinavian languages as well as English, shows how the processes of learning to read and spell are affected by the characteristics of the writing system that children are learning to master.

Children's Understanding of Biology and Health

Michael Siegal and Candida Peterson

This book uses new research and theory to present the first state-of-the-art account of children's understanding of biology and health. The international team of distinguished contributors views children's understanding in these areas to be to some extent adaptive to their well-being and survival and uses evidence collected through a variety of different techniques to consider whether young children are capable of basic theorising and understanding of health and illness. Topics ranging from babies to the elderly including birth, death, contamination and contagion, food and pain are examined and close links between research and practice are made with obvious attendant benefits in terms of education and communication.